Consciousness

Key Concepts in Philosophy

Consciousness

Josh Weisberg

polity

First published in 2014 by Polity Press

Polity Press
65 Bridge Street
Cambridge CB2 1UR, UK

Polity Press
350 Main Street
Malden, MA 02148, USA

ISBN-13: 978-0-7456-5344-0
ISBN-13: 978-0-7456-5345-7(pb)

A catalogue record for this book is available from the British Library.

Typeset in 10.5 on 12 pt Sabon
by Toppan Best-set Premedia Limited
Printed and bound in Great Britain by T.J. International Ltd, Padstow, Cornwall

The publisher has used its best endeavours to ensure that the URLs for external websites referred to in this book are correct and active at the time of going to press. However, the publisher has no responsibility for the websites and can make no guarantee that a site will remain live or that the content is or will remain appropriate.

Every effort has been made to trace all copyright holders, but if any have been inadvertently overlooked the publisher will be pleased to include any necessary credits in any subsequent reprint or edition.

For further information on Polity, visit our website: politybooks.com

For Ashley, for everything

Contents

Acknowledgments

Most of what I know about serious philosophy, and especially about the problem of consciousness, I learned from
David Rosenthal. My sincere thanks to David for all his guid-
ance; this book would not exist without him. Also, I've
greatly benefited from the work of two of the best folk
working on consciousness today: Ned Block and David
Chalmers. Ned and Dave, both in their writings and in
person, have challenged my own thinking on these issues and
this has done much to improve the quality of the material
herein.

My thinking on consciousness has been deeply shaped by
an ongoing (and sometimes drunken) debate I've been carrying out for years with Pete Mandik, Uriah Kriegel, Richard
Brown, Ken Williford, and Dave Beisecker, among many
others. It still amazes me that we get paid to do what we do,
as we'd be doing it anyway, so long as there's a place where
we can gather for beers and people don't mind us yelling
about swamp zombies and hyper-encephalated squirrels.
Thanks as well to the CUNY Cognitive Science lecture series
(run by David Rosenthal) for all the incredible talks and
discussions late into the New York night.

Thanks to my wonderful colleagues at the University of
Houston, especially Jim Garson and David Phillips who
gave me advice and encouragement as this process moved
forward. Thanks to Tamler Sommers for food, football, and

philosophy. Thanks to Cynthia Freeland for the cookies and conversation. And thanks to Bredo Johnsen for . . . well, just for being Bredo Johnsen! It is truly a gift in life when you love coming to work every day.

I presented versions of this material three times to graduate seminars at UH, and each time I received excellent feedback and advice. Many thanks to those students for their energy and enthusiasm. I also benefited immensely from co-teaching a workshop on philosophical theories of consciousness with Uriah Kriegel at the "Towards a Science of Consciousness" conference in Tucson in 2010 and 2012. Thanks to Uriah for that and all the wonderful conversations we've had over the years.

Thanks to my editor, Emma Hutchinson, and Pascal Porcheron and David Winters, at Polity Press. Emma's sure hand has made this process easy from the very beginning. Cheers! And thanks to Ken Williford who read the whole draft and provided excellent comments and criticisms, as well as insightful help in the proper use of umlauts.

Since taking on this book project, my sons Winston and Franklin were born. I love them with all my heart, but they are a handful, to say the least! Therefore it would have been impossible to write this book without the help of my friends and family. Thanks especially to Clint and Amy Harris, for Friday night cul-de-sac and more, and to my in-laws, Farrell and Peggy Hope, who have swooped in to the rescue multiple times! My mother Judy Weisberg and my late father Robert Weisberg have been incredibly supportive throughout my life – they always made me feel I could do anything and that I should follow my heart. Thanks, mom and dad! But none of this happens without the endless love and encouragement (and wisdom and backbone and childlike joy) that I've received from my wonderful wife, Ashley Hope. Truly my better half. This book is dedicated to her.

1
The Problem

What is *the* problem of consciousness? If there's one most pressing worry about consciousness in contemporary philosophy, it's what philosopher David Chalmers calls "the hard problem" (Chalmers 1996). It's the problem of explaining why anything physical is conscious at all. More specifically, why do certain physical brain processes result in the subjective experience of color, rather than experiences of sound or no experiences whatsoever? The problem is a version of an older philosophical conundrum, the so-called "mind–body problem," famous from the work of René Descartes. The hard problem of consciousness is where much of the fighting over the mind–body problem ends up after the rise of modern psychology, cognitive science, and neuroscience. Consciousness seems to be the remaining bit that fails to fit nicely into the modern scientific worldview. Even after we've explained all of what the brain does, down to the finest neural detail, the hard problem of consciousness appears unanswered. The hard problem, and philosophers' attempts to deal with it, is the main focus of this book.

But what *is* consciousness? As with many philosophical questions, even agreeing on the thing we disagree about is difficult! How we pick out consciousness in the first place can have big implications for how hard the hard problem appears. If we define consciousness as "the mysterious, unknowable core of human experience," then it's not surprising that consciousness seems inexplicable. But if we define consciousness as "whatever causes our verbal reports about how we feel," then we may be defining a real mystery out of existence at the get-go. So it would be nice if we can find a way to characterize consciousness that neither builds in unsolvable mystery, nor rules it out by stacking the explanatory deck. While there isn't a single agreed-upon definition in contemporary philosophy, unfortunately, we can focus on a set of puzzling "thought experiments" – imagined scenarios where innocent-looking steps lead us to philosophical worries – to zero in on what's at issue. And while not every philosopher agrees that the thought experiments carry great meaning, all can agree that something must be said to explain the puzzlement they generate. What's more, much of the contemporary literature on the philosophical problem of consciousness at least touches on some or all of these imagined scenarios, so they are needed background knowledge for anyone wanting to go down this particular rabbit hole.

The Knowledge Argument

The first thought experiment is called the "knowledge argument" against physicalism (Jackson 1982). Physicalism is the claim that everything is ultimately made of physical stuff like atoms and nothing else. Physicalism is a central feature of the standard scientific worldview of today. The knowledge argument seems to show that consciousness cannot fit into that worldview. The thought experiment brings out an everyday *intuition* that many of us have before we get near a philosophy classroom. Intuitions are generally unarticulated beliefs or gut feelings we have about certain subjects. For example, most people feel it's wrong to kick a puppy, even if we can't really justify why that is. A key job of philosophy is exposing these underlying intuitions and investigating whether they're to be kept or thrown out as we develop a deeper understanding of a subject. The everyday intuition brought out by the knowledge argument is the idea that a person blind from birth will never really know all that sighted folk know about colors. A blind person might ask us to describe red. We can say things like "it's a feature of objects which can vary independently of shape." The blind person might say, "Oh, you mean like texture!" But we'd have to say that's not it. We might say, "Red is hot, like the sound of a trumpet." But we'd quickly recognize that there's something we can't put into informative words, something that's left out of any description we offer to our blind friend. That left-out something, whatever it is, is a key element in the problem of consciousness.[1]

The knowledge argument takes this intuition and makes a more general point about the limits of physicalism and the scientific worldview. Instead of imagining (or actually talking to!) a blind person, we are asked to imagine a super-scientist of the future. She lives in a time when all the outstanding problems of science have been solved. What's more, she has a prodigious memory and an unfailing ability to digest and understand science. In fact, she has gone through all the relevant material and knows *all* of the facts of a completed science. But this super-scientist – let's call her Mary, following Frank Jackson who introduced this story in 1982 – has been brought up in a very special environment. Everything in her world is black and white and shades of grey (perhaps this is achieved by fitting her with special lenses which make the world look like it does on a black-and-white TV set). She has never in her life seen colors. Now for the crucial intuition-tapping question: when she's finally released from her black-and-white captivity and sees a red rose for the first time, does she learn anything new? Most of us would say that she does learn something new. She learns that this is *what red looks like*, that this is *what it's like for one to see red*. This seems like a fact she couldn't have known beforehand. But given that she already knew all of the facts of science, this must be a fact beyond the reach of science, something left out of science altogether! So there are facts beyond the scientific worldview. And since science plausibly contains all the facts about physical stuff – where all the atoms are, how they interact, and so on – this new fact must be about something that isn't physical. So physicalism, which claims that, ultimately, all the facts are physical facts, must be incorrect.

And what does this tell us about consciousness? When we think about it, the fact that Mary doesn't know before her release is a fact about her (and others') experience. It is a fact about what it's like to see red *from the inside*. She already knows all the "outside" facts about red: that it's feature of the surfaces of some physical objects, that such surfaces reflect light at certain wavelengths, and so on. She even knows, in neurological terms, what happens in normal observers when they see red: cone cells on their retinas fire in a particular ratio, activity occurs in area V4 of their brains, and so on. But *none* of these scientific facts helps her to know what it's like to experience red. That is a fact about conscious experience. There's a special quality there – the "redness" of red. Philosophers label these sorts of special qualities of consciousness "qualia." Mary lacks knowledge of red qualia. And no amount of scientific information can give her that knowledge, or so it seems. There is clearly something special about conscious experience.

So are we any closer to figuring out just what the problem of consciousness is all about? From the knowledge argument, we can see that consciousness possesses special qualities, and these qualities seemingly defy description. If you haven't experienced them yourself, no amount of what philosopher David Lewis calls "book learning" will tell you (Lewis 1988). And as philosopher Ned Block says, channeling Louis Armstrong, "if you gotta ask, you're never gonna know!" (Block 1978). And if qualia can't be informatively described, then they can't be explained scientifically, or so it seems. We are left with a hard problem! Now, not all philosophers agree with this bleak assessment of consciousness, but it's hard to deny that there at least *appears* to be an explanatory puzzle here. Throughout this book, we'll consider a range of responses to the problem, from those who accept the knowledge argument and try to sketch out what must be added to our worldview to fit in consciousness, to those who argue that the argument is misleading, inconclusive, or completely invalid. Those theorists have to explain why it is that consciousness prima facie poses a problem and then explain where consciousness fits in the current physicalist worldview. But all that matters so far is that we begin to get a feel of the philosophical worry here. A second thought experiment may help to bring that worry out further.

Zombies!

This thought experiment asks us to imagine, if we can, a creature just like us in all physical respects, right down to the last atom, but lacking consciousness (Chalmers 1996). Could you, for example, have a perfect physical doppelgänger, a molecule-for-molecule twin, who nonetheless fails to be conscious? This sort of nonconscious physical twin is called a "zombie" by philosophers. Unlike the zombies in monster movies, these "philosophical zombies" look *exactly like us* from the outside. But inside "all is dark" – there is no experience at all. Consider that many of the tasks we perform repeatedly in a day can become automated, so that we can do them on "auto-pilot." For example, if I have to wash the dishes (a task I perform many times a week at our house!), I may become so lost in philosophical or football-related thought that I lose focus on the dishes and may not even be aware at all that I've finished several plates and bowls. Might it be that a zombie does *everything* on autopilot? If such a creature is merely *conceivable* – if we can form a coherent mental picture of one – that may show that consciousness is something over and above a physical process. If consciousness were nothing more than a physical process, we shouldn't even be able to imagine zombies. Or so some philosophers argue.

Consider, by contrast, trying to conceive of something physically identical to a mountain, yet somehow not being a mountain. It's hard to even figure out what this means. That's because a mountain is nothing more than a huge pile of basic physical bits. If you have all those bits arranged in the right way, you've got a mountain. That's all there is to being a mountain. Because of this, philosophers say that mountains *supervene* on physical matter. Now back to our zombie twin. Unlike the mountain, it seems that we can at least imagine a creature just like us physically but lacking consciousness. It seems that the supervenience of consciousness on physical matter is not a straightforward affair. There seems to be at least a conceptual gap between consciousness and physical stuff, in contrast to the mountain case. To take another example, imagine a molecule-for-molecule physical duplicate of yourself, doing everything that you do, but not breathing. Or walking. Again, it seems impossible to imagine what's being asked. If a creature has all the molecules we do, and it's using them to exchange oxygen and carbon dioxide with the atmosphere, then it is breathing! That's all there is to it. Likewise, if a creature shares our molecular structure and is moving in a controlled way on two legs, it's walking. So breathing and walking supervene on our physical makeup and the action of our physical systems. But that's not obviously so for consciousness. It's not clear that all there is to consciousness is the performing of some action by a physical system. And that's the problem. What *is* consciousness if it's more than just something physical? Figuring out what consciousness is seems harder than figuring out what breathing is.

And again we can focus on just what's seems to be missing in the zombie case to try to pin down just what consciousness amounts to. When we engage in certain behaviors, it *feels* a certain way to us – there is something it's like to be us, for us, as we do these things.[2] Not so for our imagined zombie twins. This "feel," this "something that it's like for us," is the feature of the mind at issue in philosophical debates about consciousness. It's the way experience feels from the inside, for us, subjectively. And due to the apparent slippage between consciousness and physical stuff, we are faced with a puzzle. Given the success of physical science in explaining how we work, we might expect that everything about us is explainable in this way. But consciousness seems to buck the trend. It may well mark the limits of natural science. There may be a special inner core of the mind, a special property of experience, lying forever beyond the reach of scientific theory. This is the problem of consciousness.

The Long-Distance Driver

Yet another thought experiment, this one far closer to home, may help get at what's at issue. Rather than imagining superscientists of the future or strange nonconscious doppelgängers, imagine (or recall, if you can) driving for a long spell down a stretch of relatively deserted highway (Armstrong 1981). If you're like me washing the dishes, you may have found that you've driven for some time while lost in thought. You then snap back to reality and focus again on the highway in front of you. While you were "out," you didn't lose control of the car (hopefully!). That means you must have taken in visual information and used it to handle the car properly. But something was missing, something that clicked back on when you noticed the road again. That something is arguably conscious experience. It's what's lacking during the autopilot moments and what returns when you're aware of the road again. Now this thought experiment doesn't generate the puzzle the others do, but that may help us to be more clear about the subject matter here. Sometimes our mental states occur consciously, sometimes they don't. Now, what does that difference amount to? And can we explain the difference in brainy terms?

Androids

Yet another way to see the problem is to think about what we'd do if we ever met a really intelligent android. Imagine a spaceship brings a visitor from outer space to our world. It can speak our language, and we eagerly converse with this being. It tells us of its home far, far away, the trials and tribulations of spaceflight, the trouble with tribbles, and so forth. At this point, we'd probably all think such a creature must be conscious. But then imagine that we notice some wires poking out from its scalp and we ask it if it's an android. Yes, it says, and dramatically pulls off its faceplate, revealing a grid of sensors, lights, gears, and circuits! At this point, are we so sure that the being is conscious in the way we are? Many people become hesitant to attribute consciousness to such a creature, once they learn it's a robot. Why is this? Well, one aspect felt to be missing is inner feelings, the emotions and sensations we experience. An intelligent android might be able to reason and remember, perhaps even better than we do. But there seems to be an open question as to whether or not the creature is conscious.

We then might wonder if there's any further test we can do to the robot to determine once and for all if it's conscious. But what could we possibly do? We might kick it in the shins and see how it reacts. But what if it yells out and starts hopping around? Can we be sure that this is because it's in pain and not just because it's following a program of avoidance and evasion? Couldn't it just be "going through the motions"? So maybe we can try to observe its electronic "brain" in action when we kick it in the shins. But again, how would this help? No doubt we'd see all sorts of complex mechanical interactions. Circuits would allow energy to flow through various processors, analyzers would process data, and motor programs and reactions would be triggered. But is there anything there to tell us that those actions, no matter how complex, are conscious? That is, is there anything to tell us that there's subjective inner experience, replete with the "ouchy" quality of pain, going on? It seems like all could go on in the absence of consciousness. And even if consciousness is there, we don't seem to know how to detect it. As you can see, consciousness is becoming rather slippery!

And note that we'd have the same exact problem even if the visitor turned out to be fully organic and not an android at all. Imagine our visitor is filled with green goo. Could that tell us if it were conscious? How? Why is gooey organic material any better than non-gooey mechanical stuff? We seem to be in the same pickle. Even if the alien told us, in English, that it is in serious pain, that it *hurts*, how do we know that it's not just saying that because of some automatic, autopiloted response, one that occurs without the kind of inner quality we feel? At this point, you may be worried that we can't even tell if another *human* is conscious! And that is a worry, called by philosophers *the problem of other minds*. But, at least in our case, we can gain some traction by noting that we're all made of the same sort of stuff, that we have the same evolutionary backgrounds, that we have relevantly similar brain structures, and so on. But still, the very fact that this sort of worry is possible *at all* shows that there's something weird about consciousness. We know it intimately in our own case – what is better known to me than my conscious pains and pleasures? But we can only attempt to infer it in others, and it looks like a space opens up for us to be wrong about its presence. Now, this is nuts. Surely I can know that you're in pain when I kick you in the shins with my cowboy boots. So it seems, but we can feel the slippage here between conscious experience and other things we do, like breathing and walking. Some philosophers take this slippage to indicate a serious metaphysical rift in reality, a place where the normal physical rules break down. Others think that, despite first (or even second or third) appearances, consciousness in the end can be roped back into the corral of science. But it will take some doing, if it can be done at all.

A Few Disclaimers, Definitions and Distinctions

I hope that you have a bit of a feel for the problem of consciousness. We will need to become more precise as we go, but the best way to really grasp the key issues is to grapple with the pros and cons of various *theories* of consciousness offered by philosophers and scientists. This is the best way to learn about any complex and controversial subject: study the back-and-forth tennis match of ideas. It's hard to understand one theory without getting a good idea of its rivals, and it's hard to know what we really think if we don't understand views opposed to ours. This task will take up the rest of the book. We'll survey theories holding that consciousness is radically different from anything else in the universe and thus requires special metaphysical maneuvering to fit into our understanding. We'll look at views that see consciousness as just another problem for science to conquer without the need for major philosophical renovations. And we'll even look at views claiming that *any* deeper understanding of consciousness is beyond us. But first we need to lay out a few helpful ideas in order to make our journey more manageable. And we'll need to say a bit about what this book is *not*. That task will take up the rest of this chapter.

While this book deals with the most persistent and central philosophical worry about consciousness, it is distinctly a work of what is loosely known as "analytic philosophy," the sort of philosophy focused deeply on issues of language and logic, an approach inspired by the work of Gottlob Frege, Bertrand Russell, Ludwig Wittgenstein, Rudolf Carnap, and others from the early and mid-part of the twentieth century. This approach, in its purest form, tries to first analyze our concepts, and then to see what those concepts, properly clarified, might pick out in the world. Using the modern logic of Frege as a central tool (amended with the modal logic of Kripke and others, from the 1960s on), analytic philosophers try to spell out exactly what our concepts, or the words that express them, mean or refer to when precisely presented in logical language. Then we see what must follow about the world (or about some possible, but nonactual world) to make those terms refer or to make sentences using those terms true. The initial grand goals of analytic philosophy, of laying out sharply just what can and cannot be said in philosophy and elsewhere, have faded, undermined by both internal and external worries (see Schwartz 2012 for a fine review of this recent history). But the basic idea of using precise logic and language to delimit philosophical problems remains. This is both a blessing and a curse. On the one hand, we arrive, when all works well, at clear, precise statements of what we're on about. On the other, there is often a fetishistic overuse of logical and quasi-logical language ("by the term 'sun' I will mean that object X, independent from any Y, orbited by planets f, g, h, . . . , i, that has the property P of being yellow, etc."), as well as an occasional descent into a scholastic investigation of pedantic trees at the expense of more interesting philosophical forests. I will do my best to emphasize the useful features of analytic philosophy and to minimize the annoying and the useless!

With that stated, it should be noted that there are other ways to approach this subject matter. One is to take what is broadly termed a "phenomenological" approach, one inspired by the work of Husserl in the early twentieth century, and work of such thinkers as Merleau-Ponty, Heidegger, Sartre, among others. While there is no easy classification of these works, they all lean to some extent on what is known as the "phenomenological method," rooted in Husserl's philosophy. Such an approach tries to "bracket" off any presuppositions about what we are in contact with in experience and to lay out just the "things" of experience themselves. What is found there and what happens next, philosophically speaking, differs greatly even among those committed to phenomenology. I will not be directly addressing this approach. This is as much for reasons of focus as anything else, and I by no means think that the phenomenological and analytic approaches must be in conflict. I see them, when done with care, as aiming at the same questions and even agreeing on much of what must be explained, even if connecting the two "camps" is not always easy. An excellent attempt to bring the two sides together is Shaun Gallagher and Dan Zahavi's *The Phenomenological Mind*. And the work of the late Francisco Varela did much to show how phenomenology and neuroscience might be usefully combined (see Varela 1996).

Further, I am not taking a distinctively neuroscientific approach to the problem of consciousness, though I will spell out some key spots where neuroscience and philosophy directly intersect. Again, this is certainly not because I think the philosophical questions are fully independent of questions in neuroscience, nor do I think neuroscience cannot alter the way philosophical issues are framed and resolved. On the contrary! But for reasons of focus, I will not even attempt to scratch the surface of the huge and ever-expanding neuroscientific literature on the conscious brain, except as it directly relates to the philosophical theories of consciousness presented herein. For an introduction to consciousness with a more neuroscientific approach, see Antti Revonsuo's *Consciousness: The Science of Subjectivity*. See also the wonderful popular works by neuroscientists Antonio Damasio, Joseph LeDoux, Michael Gazzaniga, and others. The interface between science and philosophy is extremely fluid when it comes to this topic. I hope that the current work will allow readers to usefully frame scientific results in light of philosophical controversies. And I hope the reader will still have time for minor things like eating and sleeping as well. There is just too much good stuff to read in this area, I'm afraid!

With that clarified, we can now consider some key distinctions that will pop up in the book. It is important to keep in mind that we use the word "consciousness" (and "conscious") in a number of different ways. It's vital to be clear about what we mean. Sometimes we use the word "consciousness" to say something about creatures. We say, "The patient is unconscious," or "Has the leopard regained consciousness yet?" In doing so, we are saying whether the creature is awake or unresponsive. When we get hit over the head with a tire iron, we lose consciousness in this sense. We can call this use of the word *creature consciousness*. But we also use the word to distinguish between our mental states. Some states are conscious and some are not. For example, I am currently in a conscious state of seeing my computer in front of me and of feeling my fingers as they type. But some of my states are not conscious (at least not until I mention them): my beliefs about the history of England, my desire for a new guitar, and so on. And I arguably even have nonconscious sensory states, like the state of feeling my rear end in my chair. Once I attend to it, the state becomes conscious, but before that, I keep track of my position on the chair and the pressures on my limbs nonconsciously. So some mental states are conscious and some are not. We can call this use of the word *state consciousness*.[3]

While there are some interesting exceptions, in this book we will be mainly interested in *state consciousness*. We want to know what has to be added to a mental state to make it a conscious state. We want to know if the special features that mark off conscious states from nonconscious ones are features that can be explained in physical, scientific terms. Creature consciousness, as I've defined it, is more of a basic biological function, that of being awake rather than completely unresponsive. And while we might wonder if a creature can really be creature conscious if none of its states are conscious, the real problem is about the states themselves. This is not to say, of course, that there aren't deep and fascinating questions about creature consciousness, notably surrounding the issue of persistent vegetative states and coma, but they are not the focus of our work here.

Another point about the word "consciousness" as we'll be using it in this book: the kind of consciousness that allegedly causes the problems we're interested in is sometimes called *phenomenal consciousness* in philosophy. Phenomenal consciousness is the sort of consciousness that occurs when there's "something it's like to be you – for you," to paraphrase philosopher Thomas Nagel. Some philosophers argue that phenomenal consciousness is really some easier-understood thing, while others hold that it is a special and unique phenomenon. We need to be neutral in our use of the term. All I mean by "phenomenal consciousness" is the sort of conscious experience marked by qualities like redness or painfulness, the consciousness causing the worries we touched on above. By using the term, I don't mean to endorse the idea that phenomenal consciousness is unique and special, nor do I wish to deny it. Like many technical terms in philosophy, a lot is built into the usage, so we must be careful. But because "phenomenal consciousness" has become widely used as the term picking out the thing all the fighting is about, I'll follow the herd and use it as well. So sometimes I'll say "consciousness," other times "phenomenal consciousness," and even things like "phenomenal experience." I mean the same thing by all of them: the kind of consciousness there's something it's like for the subject to experience, the consciousness that keeps philosophers up at night.

We also need to say a few preliminary words about what it means to say "everything is physical" or "consciousness is nothing more than a physical process," or "phenomenal properties are just physical properties" and so on. One way to think of the problem of consciousness is via the question of how consciousness could just be a process like digestion or respiration or perspiration. These biological processes, though there are still some things we don't know about them, seem to fit right into the scientific view that everything happening in the universe is ultimately a process involving the basic forces of nuclear attraction, electromagnetism, and gravity, in various combinations. Digestion is a process by which food is broken down into usable energy for the body. This is a chemical process: complex starches, say, are converted into the glucose our cells need to power their activities. And the chemistry is explainable in terms of more basic atomic interactions: various attractions and repulsions at the atomic level make up chemical reactions. There's nothing else to them in the final analysis. And likewise for respiration, which is a transfer of gases between body and world. And for perspiration, the release of water onto the skin, which then cools the body by evaporation. All these things are chemical processes, and the chemical processes are themselves nothing more than atomic physical processes.

The idea that *everything* in the universe is nothing more than these sorts of physical processes is called *physicalism*. Philosophers have given more precise formulations of the idea, but this gives us the basic flavor.[4] The big question about consciousness is: is it nothing more than a physical process in the same way that digestion, respiration, and perspiration are nothing more than physical processes? Another term used by philosophers to capture this question is "supervene." If one thing *supervenes* on another, then that thing is nothing over and above the thing it supervenes on. Another way of putting it is to say that if A supervenes on B, there can be no change in A without a change in B. Mountains, for example, are nothing over and above huge clumps of atoms in the right locations. When God was making mountains, all he had to do was put some huge clumps of atoms in the right places. He didn't have to do anything else once he had the atoms in place – he didn't have to add any "magic mountain dust" to transform those huge lumps of atoms into mountains. All there is to mountains is huge clumps of properly arranged atoms. So we say mountains *supervene* on huge clumps of atoms. They are nothing above and beyond that. Now, the question about consciousness becomes: does consciousness *supervene* on complex arrangements of atoms, or is there something more to it. When God lays out all the complex atoms of the brain into the correct wrinkly, folded, unbelievably intricate shape, is he done, or does he still have to add whatever it is that allows this clump of atoms to have experiences? That is the problem of consciousness.[5]

We need to get a bit clearer about one other thing before we start our investigation. Sometimes the problem of consciousness is put in *metaphysical* terms, in terms of what kind of stuff there is in the universe. We wonder if consciousness is physical stuff or something more. But there is a related and deep problem of *epistemology*, of what and how we know about consciousness. This can be put in terms of explanation: can we *explain* consciousness in physical, scientific terms, or must it be explained in some other way? Or maybe it can't be explained at all, at least not by us measly humans! We've already said a bit about the metaphysical way of seeing the problem (and we'll get into much more detail about this as we go), so we need a bit of setup for the epistemological/

explanatory side of the issue. And like most (all?) things in philosophy, this too is a matter of great debate, one that will only become clear by digging into the details of various theories. But there is a way to usefully divide up philosophical approaches to consciousness, depending on whether or not (or to what degree) they hold consciousness can be *reductively* explained.

Reductive explanation, broadly, is explaining a complex, "higher-level" thing in terms of an arrangement of simpler "lower-level" parts. A prime example of reductive explanation is the explanation of the gene in terms of bits of DNA. Genes were introduced in genetic theory as the things that carry hereditary information from parent to offspring. It was later discovered by Watson and Crick that bits of DNA actually do this work in living organisms. So we can conclude that the gene is nothing more than the relevant bits of DNA – genes, that is, are reductively explained in terms of DNA. A reductive explanation shows how a complex, high-level thing is really just the workings of a bunch of simpler, lower-level things. And by doing so, it takes what had been a seemingly unique and independent thing and shows how it's just another example of stuff we already know about. Genes are just complex chemicals, and we already have a pretty good chemical theory. We don't need a whole new theory to deal with genes and what they do. Now, this is not to say that we stopped doing genetics once the structure to DNA was uncovered. It's just to say that what's really going on in genetics involves complex biochemistry, but nothing more than that. We'll discuss this worry – that reductive explanation *eliminates* rather than explains a high-level phenomenon – in chapter 6 on functionalism. For now, though, we can use the idea of reductive explanation to sketch out a rough map of philosophical views of consciousness.

One group of theories, which we can call "strongly reductive" views, holds that consciousness, like the gene, will ultimately be fully explained in terms of the arrangement of simpler and more basic parts. These sorts of views – functionalism and some versions of representationalism – hold that consciousness itself can be broken down into something more basic. Further, they hold that when we successfully break down consciousness, we'll have an illuminating explanation, just like we do when we explain genes in terms of DNA. As we'll see when we look closely at strongly reductive theories, many find this explanatory claim to be wildly implausible. How could we possibly explain consciousness in terms of nonconscious bits? But the strong reductionists certainly have boldness (or chutzpah, as my grandmother would say) on their side. If they're right, we can solve the problem of consciousness in a head-on manner. No beating around the bush, no half-measures! So maybe the explanatory rewards are worth the risk of ridicule from other philosophers.

A second class of views can be called "weakly reductive." One weakly reductive approach is given by the identity theory, at least in some of its forms. The identity theory holds that conscious states are identical to brain states. But it rejects the need to provide an illuminating explanation of this fact. According to the weak reductionist, the reason we accept the identity claim is that it makes our world a *simpler* place. Instead of having two distinct things, we have just one. And simpler is better, right? But there's no explanatory story to be told, nothing like Watson and Crick's model of DNA showing how the molecule can carry genetic information. We end up reducing, but not reductively explaining.

The third group of views we call "nonreductive." This includes various forms of mind–body dualism, as well as less-well known views like "neutral monism" and "panpsychism." All these views share the idea that we cannot explain consciousness in terms of anything more basic – it, itself, is a foundational feature of reality, or a feature at least as basic as physical stuff. We do get a kind of explanation of consciousness out of these views. We learn how the basic feature of consciousness connects with the other features of our world, like the physical workings of our bodies. But we do not learn in more basic terms what consciousness is. We've reached the foundations when we get to consciousness, so reductive explanation is out of the question.

A final class of views denies that *any* sort of explanation, reductive or otherwise, is possible for consciousness. In its strongest form, this view, called *mysterianism*, holds that our biological limitations prevent us from grasping how consciousness and the physical world fit together. We are like squirrels trying to fathom quantum mechanics. It just isn't going to happen. We might call this sort of view "strongly nonreductive," but we've got enough terminology on our plate (we philosophers are too in love with our terms, no doubt!). I will label mysterianism a nonreductive view, though, as we'll see, some "moderate" mysterians are just biding their time until a good reductive explanation comes along.

So we've got strongly reductive views, holding that consciousness can be broken down and explained in more basic terms. We've got weakly reductive views, holding that consciousness really is something more basic, but we don't get an illuminating reductive story about that. And we've got nonreductive views, holding that we can't explain consciousness in any more basic terms, though perhaps we can explain its connections to other things. When we get to the details, we'll see that these rough categories get blurry, but they capture some of the basic motivations for the various approaches to consciousness. In what follows, I'll take the views in reverse order, going from the least reductive to the most reductive. First, we'll look in detail at mysterianism, followed by various dualist approaches. Then we'll consider neutral monism and panpsychism. Next, it's the identity theory, and then versions of functionalism and representationalism. At that point, we'll have more "isms" than we know what to do with, but, hopefully, we'll have a good outline of some of the key concepts involved in the philosophical problem of consciousness.

Further Reading

The main inspiration for presenting the problem of consciousness as I do is David Chalmers's important 1996 book *The Conscious Mind: In Search of a Fundamental Theory.* This book is required reading not just for grasping the current debate on consciousness, but also for an intro to many of the methods of contemporary "analytic metaphysics." See also Chalmers, 2010, *The Character of Consciousness*, for a more recent collection of his essays, including "Consciousness and its Place in Nature," offering a map to the theoretical terrain much like the one I'm presenting here. Other excellent books on consciousness include Daniel Dennett's 1991 *Consciousness Explained*, Joe Levine's 2001 *Purple Haze*, and Derk Pereboom's 2011 *Consciousness and the Prospects of Physicalism*. Two good edited collections on consciousness are Block, Flanagan, and Güzeldere, *The Nature of Consciousness: Philosophical Debates*; and Alter and Howell's *Consciousness and the Mind–Body Problem: A Reader*. All of these books have extensive bibliographies – there is really much too much to read in this area!

2
Mysterianism

The first view we'll look at holds that the connection between consciousness and the physical world is a mystery to us. Given our cognitive limitations, we just can't get there from here. This view has been termed "mysterianism" by philosopher Owen Flanagan (1991). It comes in two flavors: one holds that the connection between consciousness and the physical world will *never* be understood by us, and the other holds that it can't be understood by us *now*, but might be in the future. We can call these "permanent mysterianism" and "temporary mysterianism." And there are differences of opinion among temporary mysterians about just how radical a leap we must make to understand the crucial connection – some are optimistic that our current methods won't require much tinkering, while others are more pessimistic and call for a revolution in our thinking. We'll look at various versions of mysterianism in this chapter, starting with the permanent mysterianism of philosopher Colin McGinn. Then we'll look at the temporary, though pessimistic, mysterianism of philosophers Joseph Levine and Thomas Nagel. We'll close by looking at the more mild-mannered and optimistic temporary mysterianism of philosophers Patricia Churchland and Tamler Sommers.

McGinn's Permanent Mysterianism

Mysterianism, like the other approaches to consciousness we'll consider in this book, is concerned with the possibility of an illuminating explanatory connection between consciousness and the physical world, in particular with our brains. We have two very different things here, so it seems. On the one hand, we've got our conscious experiences, our aches and pains, our sensory experiences of vision and touch, our feelings of anger and joy, and so on. For the moment, we'll take it that it's very clear what we're all talking about when we refer to the things on this side of the ledger. If I have to try and explain to you what pains feel like, we won't get far here! But we can say that we know about our conscious pains in a special way. We know about them "from the inside," subjectively. We know about our own pains, so it seems, in a way others could not. Likewise, we do not know about the pains of others in this way (though we may have "sympathetic pains" when we see someone else hurting). We can call this way of knowing about our conscious states *accessing them from the first-person perspective*. We thus know of pains in a special way. But the thing we know of in this way is also special. We access a particular type of "feel," the "ouchiness" of pain. This is the quality that I begged-off of trying to put into words a moment ago. It's something we who've had pains know all too well, but we couldn't say that much about it to someone who's never felt pain. There seems to be something indescribable, or "ineffable," as philosophers say, about the quality we experience. So both the conscious pain itself and our way of getting at it subjectively seem to have unusual features.

On the other hand, we know from science (and from everyday observation) that there is a physical world filled with various things, and among these things is our own body. What's more, several hundred years of science provide us with more and more detailed and complex theories of how the physical world, including our bodies, behaves. And in the last hundred years or so, with an ever-increasing pace, science has delved into the mysteries and intricacies of the human brain. This sort of knowledge is accessible and transmittable to anyone smart enough to read and grasp the required texts. What's more, the way this knowledge has been arrived at involves public, checkable, reproducible science. Science, at its heart, is a public venture, one essentially employing a community of people working on the same sorts of problems, using the same sorts of methods. These methods require that scientific theorizing and experimentation *must* be accessible from the *third-person perspective*, from an objective (or at least intersubjective) point of view. The scientific knowledge of our bodies is objective.

And what do we learn of our bodies from science? Well, in extremely rough strokes, we learn that our bodies are evolved biochemical machines. They are entities that work by the complex push-and-pull of chemical reaction. And it seems that, at least in principle, we could learn all there is to know about our bodies by coming to fully understand the functions the body performs and how the various chemicals in us perform those functions. Obviously, this is wild exaggeration, given our current state of knowledge in biochemistry, physiology, medicine, and so on, but it seems like there's nothing deeply philosophical in the way of ever increasing our knowledge of the physical side of the ledger.

We are left, though, wondering how to square the two sides of the ledger. How could it be that the rich reds, oranges, and purples of the visual experience of a sunset *just are* some process in our physical brains? How could the one thing be no more than just the other? And how might they connect at all? The permanent mysterian holds that we will never be able to discover the true nature of this connection. We just don't have the mental moxie to do it. Explanatory failure: when your very best explanation just isn't good enough!

Colin McGinn offers an argument for the permanent mysterian position. It is based on a concept from cognitive science known as "cognitive closure." Cognitive science gives us reason to believe that our minds are decomposable, at least in part, into separate processing "modules." Modules are relatively isolated mental processors devoted to solving specific problems in a single domain. They are not used for general intelligence or problem solving. Instead, they are specific automatic mental machines, built to do one limited job only. Examples of modular processing include basic visual perception, language comprehension, and facial recognition. In order to see even a simple visual scene, we must segment the scene into figure and ground so we can pick out the key things we're seeing. To do so, we use automatic mental processes which detect lines and boundaries and eventually meaningful objects. All this happens quickly and outside of awareness. The process is seen as modular because it is relatively immune to other information we may possess. Even knowing that the lines are the same length does not alter the way the Müller-Lyer illusion looks (see Figure 2.1).

Modular processes seem isolated or "encapsulated." They just work automatically the way they do, no matter what else we may know or learn about the scene in front of us. The same holds true for language comprehension. We can't help but hear certain sounds as meaningful words, if they're spoken in a language we know. And our minds seem to see faces everywhere. We're just built that way.

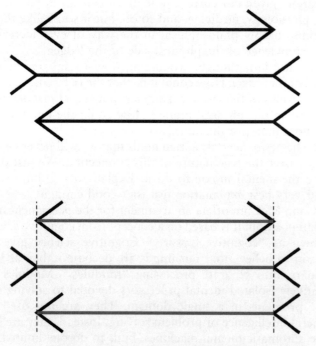

Figure 2.1 The Müller-Lyer illusion

So, if we know that some mental processes are modular, and so shielded from new knowledge or learning, we can reason that it might turn out that our minds overall have a similar kind of encapsulated limit. We just may not be built to understand the real connection between conscious experience and the physical brain. In the same way that knowledge of the real line lengths doesn't change how the Müller-Lyer illusion looks, if we somehow received the true story of the consciousness–brain connection, it wouldn't change our understanding. We may be cognitively closed to that information. That is, we may be no better than squirrels trying to grasp quantum mechanics. Try as we might, it isn't going to happen, and no amount of philosophical or scientific advancement is going to change that.

McGinn doesn't leave it at that. Sure, it may be a possibility that we're "cognitively closed" in this way, but why think that's really what's happening? McGinn tries to close off the exits with the following argument, an argument listing off the ways we might come to know about the link and rejecting each of these ways (McGinn 1999).

1 To really understand the link between consciousness and brain, we must rely on either introspection, perception, or an inference based on perception.
2 None of these methods allows us to really understand the link.
3 So we'll never really understand the link.

We know about our conscious states by way of introspection. But introspection tells us nothing about the brain. For all we know introspectively, we might not even have brains! So, because it is silent about one side of the ledger, it can't tell us how the two sides are connected. Perception falls short from the other side. We know about our brains from perceptual observation in science. But we cannot perceptually observe our conscious experiences. For all I can tell from the outside, looking at a brain, there might not be any experiences going on in there at all. So, because it, too, is silent about one side of the ledger, perception can't tell us about the connection. But what about an inference based on perception, or more to the point, an inference based upon the theories and observations of science? This too isn't up to the job, according to McGinn, for reasons that will come up several times in the chapters that follow on dualism and "neutral monism." Science, according to this picture, only tells us about causal-mechanical processes: the push and pull of various forces and particles (or chemical bonds and reactions, etc.). There is nothing in there about what a sunset *looks like to a conscious subject*. So we can't infer something about consciousness from perceptually based science because there's just nothing like that in there to extract. But perhaps we can reason by analogy or by providing a kind of descriptive model to our scientific theory. We say that subatomic particles are like little billiard balls or spinning tops. Or we say that certain chemical bonds are like coiled springs. This gives us reason to think that, if those theories or models are effective, particles or chemical bonds really are this way. But McGinn counters that we have nothing to serve as the analogy. Whereas atoms might be like billiard balls, what are conscious experiences (or elements of conscious experiences) like, in this sense? What can we propose by way of analogy here? McGinn contends that all we have to offer are physical things and they can't do the job. We're left as in the dark as when we started. And there seems to be no other way out of the conundrum!

But this is what we should expect, say the permanent mysterians, if we're cognitively closed to the facts about the connection. We can take some comfort from this perhaps. We don't know, but we know *why* we don't know. (This form of reasoning didn't make me feel any better when I failed out of calculus, alas!) And what's more, McGinn argues that we have independent reasons to think that consciousness is indeed something physical. After all, everything else we know about seems to be, and it would be surprising if consciousness proved to be the only exception. And consciousness does seem to cause things to happen in my body – how could that occur if consciousness weren't a physical thing? We should just chill out about the desperate philosophical need to know everything about everything! A little epistemic modesty wouldn't hurt. So we can't know it all. Fine. Let's move on to more tractable things.

McGinn's permanent mysterianism hasn't stemmed the tide of philosophical and scientific theories of consciousness.

In fact, the view is usually dismissed rather quickly and without much counterargument. But this is because McGinn is in the logically unenviable position of trying to prove a certain type of negative conclusion, to prove that we'll never get somewhere, given our makeup. For one, it just seems that humans can't help themselves but to pursue the tough ones – life is just more fun that way! But the history of these negative arguments based on our current shortcomings is not a great one (see Churchland, below). It's very hard to tell, from what we don't know now, what we won't know later. In a less tongue-twister-ish phrasing, current failure doesn't reliably predict future failure. At the turn of the twentieth century, some philosophers argued we'd never understand the link between atomic structure and higher-level chemical properties. But these folks, called "emergentists," were incorrect. Likewise, science has overcome any number of troubling "anomalies" in its history. Could we really tell if was possible to develop Einstein's theory *before Einstein*? Could an ancient Greek, in his own time-period, really judge the likelihood of the development of modern chemistry? How in the world could one tell? It reminds one of the "proof" that machine-powered flight was impossible just before the Wright brothers success, or the "proof" that humans couldn't run a four-minute mile prior to Bannister's triumph. Arguments from our limitations have a poor track record.

But isn't there more to McGinn than a simple argument from ignorance? Here, McGinn does suffer from some neglect, but the key issues are the focus of debate elsewhere.[1] We'll say more when we look at dualism and other nonreductive approaches, but the main point is either to challenge the claims of what introspection brings us or to show that McGinn has downplayed the perceptual side of things. Perhaps introspection doesn't positively rule out a connection in the way McGinn suggests – it may be more neutral on what it shows. If so, it may be that the connection is less difficult to make out. Perhaps conscious states are representational states of a certain kind – states that tell us about the world in a certain way – and these can be more easily mapped to physical processes. Or maybe introspection is downright *misleading* about consciousness. Perhaps consciousness is a physical process, but it doesn't *seem* that way introspectively.

Various strongly reductive views offer rebuttals to the idea that introspection reliably presents us with something obviously disconnected from the physical. And in the other direction, it may be that we can develop a physical idea of consciousness, from the outside. Perhaps McGinn is overly restrictive about what the physical side has access to, and, once we properly expand that space, we'll see how the connection might be made. And finally, who knows what another hundred (or thousand!) years of science will bring? The real Einstein of the mind hasn't arrived yet, but when she does, she may offer a theory undreamt of in McGinn's philosophy, one that properly illuminates the allegedly closed connection.

Pessimistic Temporary Mysterianism

But there are other, more moderate versions of mysterianism. These views agree that at present we have no idea about the connection between brain and consciousness, but hold that nothing in principle precludes a "conceptual revolution," one showing how consciousness is really brainy stuff after all. But, prior to the revolution, we're in no better epistemic position than an ancient philosopher wondering about the modern claim that matter is energy, as philosopher Thomas Nagel puts it (1974: 447). Nagel is a "pessimistic temporary mysterian," someone holding that our ignorance about the link between consciousness and brain, though profound, *may* be temporary. Another philosopher defending this position is philosopher Joseph Levine. Levine (2001) argues that we have good reason to think that consciousness is a physical process in the brain. This best explains how our conscious thoughts, feelings, and emotions cause our bodily behavior. For example, I consciously feel hungry and so consciously decide to get some BBQ. This causes me to jump in my car and go to my favorite BBQ location. If consciousness isn't physical, we have no plausible story about how this sort of effect can take place. My body is a physical system and it's just not clear how something nonphysical could get it to move. Indeed, this worry – that nonphysical consciousness can't cause behavior – is one of the main stumbling blocks for dualism (see chapter 3).

But even though we have good reason to accept that mental causation demands that consciousness is physical, we have no idea *how* this could be so. We are stuck with what philosopher Immanuel Kant called an "antinomy," a puzzle where two reasonable propositions lead to an incoherent or contradictory conclusion. Both Nagel and Levine offer support for their charge of mystery by arguing for what Levine calls "the explanatory gap." The explanatory gap arguably exists between our understanding of consciousness and every physical theory we have. No matter how much we learn about the physical makeup of a creature, we still do not know what it's like to be that creature – *for* the creature. We've met this worry in chapter 1 above and it is a central point of contention in the study of consciousness. Both Nagel and Levine think that the gap shows the failure of all our current theories of consciousness. The theories are trying to explain subjective "what it's like" facts in objective, third-personal terms. What's more, they hold that *any* extension of these sorts of theories – theories using the same sorts of mechanistic tools as employed in current science – inevitably falls short as well. But, as noted, they both accept that we have good reason to hold that consciousness is nonetheless physical and, further, that we lack a compelling reason to think that our current state of ignorance is fundamentally incurable, as McGinn argues. They are thus temporary mysterians. Only a full-blown conceptual revolution can help us here, but that isn't ruled out as of yet.

But why should we think that solving the mystery here requires a revolutionary reordering of our concepts? Nagel famously makes his point by focusing on bats. In principle, we can learn all about bats from science. We can know that they use a sonar-like system of sound and hearing to navigate and hunt at night, even in pitch-black caves. We may come to know all about how the bat's brain processes these echo-location signals, how it then generates the appropriate movements and course corrections and so forth. We may even come to know how the neurons in the bat's brain underwrite these amazingly complex processes. But something will inevitably be left out of such a story: what it's like to be the bat as all this complex machinery whirrs away. What it's like *for the bat*, from the "inside." And it's not enough for us to imagine what it would be like for us to chirp and flap our arms to fly around a room at night – that would (perhaps) tell us what it would be like for *us* to be the bat. Nagel wants to know what it's like *for the bat* to be the bat! And that, so it seems, is something no amount of additional scientific information could tell us, at least as science is configured at present. There is a gap between our scientific knowledge and our knowledge of the "phenomenal facts," of facts about what it's like for the subject.

Levine offers a similar line of argument. He holds that a good explanation is one that allows us to *deduce* the phenomenon to be explained from the explanation. For example, consider the theory that tells us that water is nothing more than H_2O molecules. Knowing this, we gain an explanation of a variety of facts, like the fact that water boils at 100°C. This fact is explained by the motions and interactions of H_2O molecules as they are heated. When the heat reaches 100°C, certain bonds break, turning the liquid turns into a gas. If we accept this picture, we can deduce that water boils when heated to 100°C, because H_2O boils at 100°C and water is H_2O – there is no room left for anything else to occur. All the relevant details seem to be in place. But in consciousness's case, there are still open questions, even if we accept the idea that consciousness is nothing more than a brain process. We can still ask *why* does this brain process feel this way to the subject? Why is this what it's like for her, rather than another way or no way at all? It seems these questions are as open as when we started. In the water cases, the meaningful questions are shut off. In the consciousness case, they remain. This is what Levine calls the explanatory gap.

Still, as noted, Nagel and Levine retain some small degree of explanatory optimism. Nagel remarks,

> It may be possible to approach the gap between subjective and objective from another direction. Setting aside temporarily the relation between the mind and the brain, we can pursue a more objective understanding of the mental in its own right . . . This should be regarded as a challenge to form new concepts and devise a new method – an objective

phenomenology not dependent on empathy or the imagination. (1974: 449)

We have been in situations of seemingly intractable ignorance before, but eventually the light of explanation shone in. Perhaps our distant progeny will look back and laugh at our inability to see what they've come to grasp. Levine also keeps hope alive: "I don't expect . . . to convince anyone who is interested in pursuing [radical] alternatives that there is no prospect of success. Perhaps there is a way to make them work; if so, there clearly is a need for further research in that direction" (2001: 177). So you're saying there's a chance! This may be a very thin reed, but it's something to grasp at.

But there is a more optimistic form of temporary mysterianism, one that offers a way to perhaps blunt the arguments leading Nagel and Levine to pessimism. Instead of saying that the connection between consciousness and the brain is so mysterious that we'll never arrive at an explanation, this approach says that we don't yet know enough about the brain to be sure consciousness *can't* be explained in brainy terms. This puts the brakes on the various thought experiments offered by pessimists mentioned above. If we don't yet know all (or much) of what there is to know about the brain – and it is, after all, pretty much the most complex thing we've encountered – then how can we be sure that zombies aren't impossible and that Mary the super-scientist would in fact know all there is to know about consciously seeing red in her black-and-white room prior to her release? This is clearly an optimistic form of mysterianism: the mystery means there's still a chance of success here. We don't know enough to know we *can't* do it! What's more, the philosophers defending this sort of view tend to think there's no reason to think we won't explain everything in non-revolutionary terms one day. Ignorance is bliss indeed.

Optimistic Temporary Mysterianism

Philosopher Patricia Churchland defends a version of optimistic temporary mysterianism (Churchland 1996). She considers the zombie and knowledge arguments and notes that such claims are really just hidden "arguments from ignorance." Such arguments hold that, because we can't understand at present how consciousness could be a brainy process, we'll never understand it. As we saw above, the history of such arguments is not a good one, particularly when we look at science. Churchland mentions that when she learned high-school biology, her teacher told the class that mere chemistry alone would never explain life. This view is known in biology as "vitalism" and it was a serious theoretical contender up through the middle of the twentieth century. But its rival, "mechanism," eventually won the day and now vitalism is widely seen as a failed theory. Churchland draws a parallel between defenders of vitalism before the establishment of mechanism and defenders of dualism (and pessimistic mysterianism) at present. She argues that, for all we can tell, the defenders of dualism are in no better position than the vitalists. We have no good reason to think that science has figured out all there is to know about the brain and therefore has failed to explain consciousness. Give us another few years (or centuries, given the complexity of the task!) and then come back and appraise the anti-physicalist arguments. For all we know, neuroscience may explain the consciousness just as mechanistic biology came to explain life. Our current failure to grasp the connection may not be a good guide to what we'll grasp in the future.

Churchland provides a more detailed analysis of anti-physicalist arguments. She contends that they subscribe to the "left out" hypothesis – the idea that, no matter how much we say in third-personal, scientific terms about consciousness, something will always be *left out*, namely the feel of consciousness, what it's like for the subject. And this is just how Nagel and Levine argue above. But how, Churchland asks, can we be so sure of this if we don't yet know what the third-personal, scientific story is going to say? What's more, Churchland notes that philosophers often exaggerate how much we know about the brain on the physical side of the ledger. Problems on this side are labeled as "easy problems" by David Chalmers, for example (1996). But there are a great range of things we don't understand about the brain and this is not merely a matter of filling in details. We really don't know very much about this organ, with its *billions* of neurons with *trillions* of connections. Who knows what theoretical and conceptual advances we'll make when we move even a little way towards solving the "easy" problems? And how do we know that such changes won't make it clear that *nothing* is left out of the scientific picture? So there is indeed mystery here at present, but that should just inspire us to do more brain science, not to guillotine our current worldview.

Another version of this optimistic flavor of mysterianism is offered by philosopher Tamler Sommers (2002). Sommers notes that anti-physicalist arguments like the zombie and knowledge arguments require that we can isolate a stable meaning for the term "consciousness," one that allows us to consider if consciousness, so defined, might be absent in zombies, unknown by Mary, and so on. But how can we be so sure that we can isolate a definition of "consciousness" in this way? And what makes us think that the "isolation" is immune to influence from the sciences? Indeed, it has often been the case that our everyday understanding of things is deeply influenced by advances in the sciences. It is common knowledge that our genetics is determined by our DNA and our thinking about heredity is sensitive to this scientific claim. Perhaps as scientific knowledge of the brain advances, our *everyday* concept of consciousness will alter as well. And to be honest, how many of us can really say we've got such a solid grasp of consciousness, anyway? Are we *really* so sure we know it so well? Having taught about this issue for years, I'm well aware that one of my first tasks is explaining what consciousness is. And students don't always understand what the heck I'm on about! They then complain that I've taught them a concept of consciousness carrying with it certain perplexities. And then I rattle on about the perplexities! Sommers points out that we may know less about consciousness "from the inside" than philosophers suppose, and, what's more, what we know in that way may be less immune to change in the face of scientific advance than we realize. Taken together, we get a nice statement of optimistic mysterianism: "I don't yet know enough about consciousness to make any real substantive claim about it. But it is probably physical, as materialism is probably true, given its past success in explaining things that were once deemed 'utterly mysterious' " (Sommers

2002: 13). For all we know today, science may show us that consciousness really is fully explicable in physical terms. And it may do so, in part, by clarifying just what consciousness *is* in the first place. We don't yet know what science will do in this regard, but it has done things like this before. Thus, it's premature to hold that there's a special problem of consciousness resisting solution by non-revolutionary advances of our current science.

Conclusion: A Modest Proposal?

Mysterianism in all its forms recommends that we cool our jets in the face of the mystery of consciousness. It may be that we just don't have what it takes, now or ever, to explain how consciousness and the brain are connected. Or maybe we just don't know what wonders science will bring us in the future, so there's no need to get stressed about today's (perhaps only apparent) philosophical problems. We should occupy ourselves more productively in the meantime. But this modest proposal hasn't been embraced by most philosophers, perhaps unsurprisingly. Some take the message of the mystery to be that we need to radically rethink our basic worldview *now*. What we learn from the explanatory gap, according to these thinkers, is that consciousness is not now nor has it ever been a physical thing. Perhaps it is something ontologically distinct, that is, something in its own independent metaphysical category. This view, a venerable one in philosophy, is known as "mind–body dualism." There are a number of ways to be a dualist about conscious experience, and we'll survey some of them in the next chapter. But it may be that consciousness is not properly speaking a separate and *independent* feature reality. Instead, there may some basic stuff underlying both the physical world and the world of experience, some deeper "neutral" substance from which all other features emerge. This view is called "neutral monism." Or perhaps everything in reality is both physical and phenomenal – there is a little bit of consciousness in everything. This view is called "panpsychism." These nonreductive views claim to be distinct from mind–body dualism, but they also reject the possibility of reducing consciousness to the physical. We will look at a range of these complex metaphysical positions two chapters from now.

All these nonreductive views take the *epistemic* mystery of consciousness to entail important things for the *metaphysics* of consciousness. They differ in exactly how they fit consciousness into the world, but they agree that the mystery can't be solved by following the usual route of reductive physical science. Instead, we need to add something to our *ontology*, our score sheet of what there is in reality. By contrast, reductive views, including the identity theory, functionalism, and representationalism, all take the optimistic mysterians to have correctly located the meaning of the mystery, but they take the bolder, less modest step of actually trying to develop theories of consciousness *now*! Some of the views hold that they are helping in the process suggested by Churchland – they are participating in a broadly construed scientific project, and success in this project will eventually show that the gap can be closed. Others take Sommers's point about meaning to heart and hold that we may have an incomplete or even erroneous idea of consciousness in the first place. These theorists try to highlight the confusions implicit in our everyday, "inner" idea of consciousness and they bring out how thinking about consciousness in a functionalist or representationalist way, for example, can show how there is less to the mystery than is often thought. Further, as we connect all the dots between reductive philosophical and psychological theory, neuroscience, and perhaps fields like artificial intelligence, biology, and even physics, it may become clear that nothing is left out and that worrying about zombies is stupid. The second half of the book will take up these views. So there may be mystery at present, but just what we should make of this mystery is fully up for grabs. And philosophers have lots of bold, immodest conjectures about the right way to proceed. But that's really not surprising: philosophers never were much good at modesty of any kind!

Further Reading

McGinn's main text on this issue is his 1999 *The Mysterious Flame*. Nagel's view, which involves much more than just consciousness, is spelled out in his 1986 *The View from*

Nowhere. See also his more recent *Mind and Cosmos*. Levine's 2001 *Purple Haze* presents his view and more besides. Finally, Churchland's *Neurophilosophy* is an excellent introduction to her work, as well as a sort of manifesto on how to bring neuroscience into the philosophical debate on consciousness. See also Flanagan (1991).

3
Dualism

A famous response to the mystery surrounding consciousness is to conclude that consciousness is not something physical, that it is a fundamentally different type of thing. This view is called *dualism* and its most famous champion is René Descartes, the father of modern philosophy.[1] Descartes argued for a dualism of *mind* and body, but he thought that mentality and consciousness always went together. And lots of what he said about mind applies equally well to more restricted discussions of consciousness. Indeed, some of the specific dualist arguments he used are still with us today, though in modernized versions. However, there's a major difference between Descartes's dualism and its more modern forms. Descartes was a *substance* dualist: he thought that the mind was a kind of "stuff" capable of existing completely independently of any physical stuff.

"Substance" is a "philosopher's word," like "property," "object," "state," or "event." These words have a normal meaning in everyday talk, but in the mouths of philosophers they become highly abstracted and technical. Take "substance," for example. I might say, "There is a strange orange substance on the couch." And I may look accusingly at my two-year-old son. We all have a good idea what I mean by "substance": whatever that goo is staining the sofa. But when philosophers use "substance," they mean the most basic and underlying stuff, the stuff that goes through changes and yet somehow remains underneath. An egg may turn into a chicken, which turns into dinner, which turns into fat around my midriff. There is something that went through these changes, which altered as it went. And that stuff is neither egg nor chicken nor nugget. Substance is the underlying stuff that wears the various "clothes" we see: the "properties" it possesses at various times. But it is something separate from any of these clothing properties. So what, exactly, is it? This has perplexed philosophers since Aristotle introduced the idea. John Locke thought we couldn't say anything about it, but it must be there: it is "a thing we know not what."[2] And yet philosophers have argued and continue to argue about substance. And the problem with "philosopher's words" is not limited to "substance." The same sorts of problems of "hyper-abstraction" lurk around terms like "object," "state," "entity," and so on. What *is* an object exactly? What do all objects have in common? This is not to say that philosophers haven't offered answers to these questions, nor is it to say that all philosophical debate is inherently confused or muddled. I just want to flag these sorts of terms (indeed, we've been using lots of them already!) because they sometimes carry lots of hidden implications and unexpressed assumptions. Caveat, Lector! Reader, beware!

Now back to Descartes's substance dualism. He holds that there are two fundamental kinds of stuff, two kinds of underlying goo that can exist on their own: minds and bodies. By "bodies," he meant all physical matter. And by "minds," he meant consciously thinking things. This had the advantage of carving out a place for religion in the new scientific worldview. Physical body would be the province of science – a place where everything can be explained by mechanistic scientific theory, a theory explaining how the push and pull of basic entities and forces accounts for all we can see. Mind, on the other hand, exists independently of these forces. It is not the sort of thing that can get caught by the net of mechanistic causal law. It stands outside of the physical nexus. And this opens up the space for the mind to survive the death of the body; for the mind to decide what to do free of the laws of physics, chemistry, biology, etc.; and for the mind to do those amazing things, such as reason, imagine, create, and feel, that it does in ways no machine could.

One of the arguments offered by Descartes for his dualism is worth revisiting because of its similarity to some current ways of arguing for dualism. Descartes claimed that, because he could clearly and distinctly *conceive* of his mind without his body, the two really are distinct, as God guarantees the truth of anything clearly and distinctly conceived. Descartes's invocation of this "divine guarantee" of clear and distinct ideas was objected to in his own day and is generally rejected today, even by those believing in God. But the style of arguing, from what we can conceive or imagine to what really must be, is alive and well. As we'll see shortly, a major proponent of modern-day dualism, David Chalmers, employs this sort of reasoning, bringing in his famous *zombies*, mentioned in chapter 1. Indeed, this really is the main issue with consciousness perhaps. We just cannot see how it connects with anything else! It seems easy to imagine it occurring without any body or brain or what have you. But this alone only gets us mysterianism. We need something to connect the conceiving or imagining with the real world. Descartes leans on God's non-deceiving goodness to provide the link. He argued that God, being all good, is not a deceiver, and to let me be deceived about things I grasp so completely and clearly would be – well – mean. And God is not that sort of being. So clear and distinct ideas are guaranteed to be true. But if we fail to follow Descartes in his theistic reasoning, we need to find another way to link the epistemic mystery of consciousness to an actual dualism of consciousness and physical reality.

From Substance to Property Dualism

Several key developments have occurred in the debate since Descartes's day. For one, we no longer look for the sort of infallible certainty Descartes demanded in his epistemology. Rather, we fallibly try to find the best set of reasons and evidence we can to bring to bear on a problem and go from there. Also, since the development of modern logic and computers, it's widely held that there's a decent solution to the problem of explaining how any physical thing could *reason*. Computers, it appears, may be able to reason, if not today then sometime in the not-too-distant future. And this provides a story about how a physical machine could be rational and logical. This would no doubt have impressed Descartes, with his appreciation of both the power of reason and the subtlety of mechanism and machines. But this leaves the question of consciousness wide open. While it may be that a machine can reason, it seems as mysterious as ever how a machine could feel pain or savor the taste of good BBQ. What's more, while Descartes was motivated to prove the existence of mind as a separate substance, modern philosophy is concerned instead with the possibility of a dualism of *properties*.[3] The focus on properties results in part from a shift in thinking about the mind, from the idea that the mind is an independent thing to the idea that the mind is a collection of states a person can be in at one time or another.

One of the factors moving us from substances to states is the behaviorist idea that mind might be best thought of as a way that the body behaves. We can act unthinkingly or intelligently. We can react happily or disgustedly. These ways of being are recognizable by others. The behaviorists held that it was crucial that our mental words must be publicly "checkable" if they were to make sense at all. This led them to the radical conclusion that mental words simply picked out groups of actual and potential behaviors. They picked out ways the body behaves. Thus, we arrive at the idea of mental states. States are best understood by example: a smile is a state my mouth can be in. It is not something separate from and independent of my mouth. It can't float off on its own, despite what Lewis Carroll suggests with his Cheshire cat. Likewise, on this view, we should think of mind in terms of mental states. These are ways the person can be – states the person can be in. And there's no obvious reason to think that mental states are anything more than states of a physical body.

Behaviorism fell by the wayside in philosophy and psychology to be replaced by *functionalism*, the view that mental stuff can be defined in terms of what it does, not what it's made out of. And one of the key thing minds do is *compute*: they take information from the senses, transform it in various ways, and trigger the behavior best suited to meet the organism's goals. Thus, we get the *computer theory of mind*, the idea that the mind is a computer. But the state idea is retained, and we arrive at the modern view that mental states are computational states. And we have a good idea how a physical system could be in computational states because we know how to make computers of ever-increasing complexity and power. So physicalism about the mind looks promising! Further, we can move beyond the narrow confines of behaviorism and talk about inner mental states as inner computational states. What could be wrong with that?[4]

Here the modern-day dualist jumps in. Sure, mental states may in the main be computational states, but they are more than just that. They are marked by certain *properties* beyond those needed for the functionalist job of computing. These properties are *phenomenal properties*, properties defined by how they "feel" to the subject. Properties like the painful slice of a paper cut or the shimmering reddish and golden highlights of the experience of a sunset. What are properties, you ask? Good question. They are the features of things, the attributes that distinguish them from other things. Properties are repeatable features of objects: more than one thing can be reddish or painful. They are picked out by our predicates: we speak of a *red* ball or a *juicy* BBQ brisket. "Red" and "juicy" pick out properties, of balls and briskets, respectively. What more can we say about properties? Not much, without opening a rather unpleasant philosophical can of worms. For example, do properties exist independently of objects? Can we give clear "existence conditions" for them? Are there properties we do not (and cannot?) have predicates for? All this may not matter too much to get the feel of modern property dualism, but it's worth remembering that "property" is a philosopher's word if anything is!

So where are we? We left behind the mind as substance and moved to questions of mental states. But we can now ask about the properties of mental states. And here, it seems, we find the problematic features of consciousness back with a vengeance. The philosophical rug always bumps up somewhere. But why think there are problematic properties lurking here? The zombie argument is one reason. The zombie goes as follows:

1   We can conceive of zombies, beings physically just like us but lacking consciousness.

2 If we can conceive of zombies, they are possible.
3 If zombies are possible, physicalism is false.
4 Therefore, physicalism is false.[5]

The first premise is supposed to be straightforward. It's just the epistemic gap picked out by Levine and Nagel. Nothing in our physical conception of reality guarantees that consciousness *must* be there. It seems easy enough to imagine a being satisfying our physical specifications, even though "all is dark inside." Or so it's widely assumed. But even if we grant premise one, it's premise two that provides the bridge from epistemic mystery to metaphysical reality. Why think that just because we can conceive of something that it's possible? And what does it mean to be possible in this sense, anyway? This seems to be yet another of those philosopher's words: it works well enough in everyday conversation, but it gets wobbly in the hands of philosophers.

For modern-day philosophers, something is possible when there is a *possible world* where that thing exists.[6] Possible worlds provide us with a complete description of the way things might be. It gives us an item-for-item inventory of the world, telling us where everything is. And philosophers have developed sets of rules to tell us what sorts of things can be in possible worlds and what sorts of things cannot. The crucial idea to grasp for the zombie argument is how some things rule out other things in possible worlds and how some things guarantee the presence of other things. For example, if I know that the laws of physics in a possible world are just like the laws in our actual world, then I know that light can't go faster than light speed,186,000 miles a second. And if I know that there are H_2O molecules in a world, then I know there are water molecules in that world as well, given that we know that water is just H_2O molecules. These *entailment* relations are tracked by what philosophers call *modal logic*. The zombie is a modal logic argument against the claim that consciousness is a purely physical thing.

So how does it work? David Chalmers (1996; 2010, ch. 6) argues that we ought to be able to rule out the possibility zombies if physicalism about consciousness is true. Think about an imaginary "water dualist," someone who thinks there's more to water than just H_2O molecules. We explain to her that everything that water does – how it boils at 100°C, how it freezes at 0°C, how it appears transparent, etc. – is fully explained by what H_2O molecules do. If she still insists that there's something more to water, we can ask her to imagine a world where there are lots of H_2O molecules all around, doing just what water does in our world. Is this really a world without water? It seems that it is not – all there is to water is the stuff that does just what those H_2O molecules do. Indeed, that's why we accept the claim that water is H_2O! So there's no possible world where there's H_2O and no water. Fixing where the H_2O molecules are fixes where the water is – water *supervenes* on H_2O. Further, the story about H_2O molecules, that is, our total physical theory about the nature of H_2O, tells us all there is to know about water. There are no remaining open questions.

But now consider the case of zombies. We might fix all the physical facts in a world, pin down where every last molecule is located and what it's doing, and *still* wonder if a critter made of these physical molecules is conscious. There seems to be a gap here. This indicates, according to Chalmers, that there is no entailment relation between the physical facts and the "phenomenal facts" – the facts about what it's like to be a critter. And if these entailment relations do not hold, then there can be a possible world just like ours physically but lacking consciousness. And that shows that consciousness is not physical because all physical things are fixed by these sorts of entailment connections to the basic physical stuff. So zombies aren't just conceivable, they're positively possible, in the relevant sense. And that means that physicalism about consciousness is false and dualism, the idea that there's not just physical properties but also nonphysical "phenomenal properties" as well, is true.[7]

But how can we be sure that the entailment relations don't really hold? In the water/H_2O case, we needed a full-blown scientific theory to see the connections. Indeed, there were some who worried such connections would never be found and so rejected reductive physicalism about chemical properties like the transparency of water. In response, Chalmers argues that all the usual ways of showing that the possibility is just apparent and nothing more fall short here. The real issue is that, unlike water (and perhaps everything else, other than consciousness), the phenomenal feel of conscious states can't be cashed out in terms of *doing something*. In the water example I just gave, once we knew that H_2O *does* everything that water *does*, we know that water is nothing more than H_2O. Water, it seems, is fully defined by what it does. This is called a *functional characterization* of water. Chalmers argues that there cannot be a completely functional characterization of consciousness. And because of that, we can't rule out possible worlds physically identical to ours but lacking consciousness. The problem is we can imagine doing all the things that consciousness does unconsciously. We can imagine a creature reacting and moving just as we do, but fully on "autopilot." Indeed, this is just what we're imagining when we imagine zombies. But the imagining itself here seems to block the usual way of finding the entailment relations we need – of developing a functional characterization and showing how physical stuff does the functional work. Consciousness seems to be more than the doing of something. It also has a distinctive feel or phenomenal quality. Pains do things for us. They help us to move out of the way, to avoid damage, to seek medical help. All this is doing, function. But pains also *hurt*! And that's the bit that just doesn't seem to be capturable in a functional characterization. So we can't connect the phenomenal properties of consciousness to physical stuff the way we do with other things. The mere conceivability of zombies shows that the facts of consciousness are not entailed by the physical facts. Consciousness floats free of the physical stuff, at least in metaphysical principle. It seems there is a dualism of physical and conscious properties.

There are many, many things to say in response to this argument. Some attack the usefulness of modal entailment claims in any context – that is, they deny that the identity between water and H_2O has much, if anything, to do with these sorts of modal claims.[8] Others agree that consciousness is unique but deny that this means that it isn't physical at the end of the day. And some refuse to let the whole thing get started and deny that we really can conceive of zombies.[9] Or perhaps we're confused about what consciousness is in the first place, so we can't put much weight on what we can naively conceive of. These various responses will be considered in later captures dealing with reductive physicalist views. For now, we'll take the zombie as given, and see what sort of view follows. There are two main stripes of dualism these days. Both are versions of property dualism, holding that phenomenal properties are metaphysically distinct from physical properties, but they differ about the connections between physical and phenomenal properties. The big issue is about the potential for *interaction* between the physical and the phenomenal. Those views holding that causal interaction between the two sorts of properties is possible are called "interactionist dualist" views. Those views rejecting the possibility of causal interaction are called "epiphenomenal dualist" views. We'll consider them in turn.

Interactionist Dualism

Interactionist dualists hold that consciousness must be added as a basic feature of our ontology, of our official catalog of what there is.[10] Just as electromagnetism was added as a new force to the Newtonian world of gravitational attraction, we must add consciousness as a basic element of the universe. It might be thought that this is inherently antiscientific: we're adding a mysterious new element to the well-understood forces and particles of physics. But so long as we can work out lawful connections between consciousness and everything else, we're in no worse position than when we added electromagnetism to our ontology. Or so this idea, called by Chalmers "naturalistic dualism," holds (Chalmers 1996). But there is clearly something more radical going on here. Electromagnetism can be given a functional characterization. What's more, the causal patterns of physical systems, including those involving electromagnetism, are held to be complete. The energy in such systems is conserved: no new energy comes in from outside, so to speak. This idea, known as "the causal closure of the physical," seems a fundamental and well-confirmed bit of science. Can the nonphysical properties of consciousness fit into our worldview in the same way?

It seems to many that they cannot. When we think about the human body and its behaviors, it looks like we can explain everything it does in terms of prior *physical* causes.[11] We just do not need to bring in anything else. And we don't find any extra bolt of energy coming in from outside. As we watch the brain go through its various complex patterns, at → no point do we see a burst of additional "mental energy" indicative of consciousness making things happen in the brain. So it seems that there's no place for consciousness to cause anything in the brain. Now, this is a very odd conclusion, as we'll stress in the section below on *epiphenomenal* dualism. But to reject the conclusion is to reject the principle of the causal closure of the physical and to hold that, upon closer examination, there really is consciousness to brain causation. What can be said in favor of this view?

First, it's not so clear that causal closure is really the be-all and end-all of physical science.[12] Both relativity theory and quantum mechanics, our two most advanced physical theories, may not require closure. When thinking about the fixed models of Galileo and Newton, closure seems crucial, but in today's physics, things are much more complex. And even more so when we look at the brain. The incredible complexity of the interwoven networks of neurons in the brain opens up plenty of space for consciousness to have a causal influence. Given the firing of some huge set of neurons, all we can predict is that with some degree of probability some future pattern will emerge. But in this complex morass of interacting neurons, there may well be subtle influences from consciousness. The statistical regularities are not fully deterministic in their evolution. That is, things are pretty "chaotic" in the brain, mathematically speaking. A small perturbation by phenomenal properties may have a big effect downstream, without overturning the applecart of science. So, when we look closely at the causation in the brain, the messiness of it all opens the door for interactive dualism. So long as we're not looking for big bolts of change outside the range of accepted probabilities, there's no straightforward reason to hold that brain science rules out interaction.

And the case for interaction gets a further boost from the inherent weirdness of quantum mechanics. This isn't the greatest prop to lean on: arguments relying on an interpretation of quantum mechanics (QM) are extremely controversial, given how hard it is to grasp just what to make of this most powerful and least comprehensible of our theories.[13] But on some interpretations of QM, to get the stable "classical" reality we observe – rather than the overlaid pattern of probabilities of the quantum world – we need *observation* to occur. Before any "looking" happens, there's just a spread of things that are more or less probable, all of which in some way are real. But once someone looks, the pattern of probabilities "collapses" into the one "actual" event we see. The coin comes up heads. The cat dies. Whatever. But before the looking, the coin was both heads and tails and the cat both lived and died. Alright, this is truly bizarre, so weird that even as creative a mind as Einstein's couldn't fathom it. But if we accept this sort of reading of QM, what are we to make of the looking, the observing? Here may well be a special and indeed central role for consciousness. It may be the thing outside of the quantum flux that does the looking. And maybe without consciousness, there'd be no stable reality to begin with. Perhaps consciousness decides to look at this or that, and that initiates the process of collapse resulting in the one actual event that we see. This is a kind of interaction: consciousness is outside the physical system it observes and then causes that system to collapse from the range of probable states defined by QM into the one we see in classically described reality.

Further, it may be that the kinds of things a conscious mind can do, the creative fire and the out-of-the-box leaps, can't be explained by a classical computing system. There are arguments in mathematical logic suggesting that any computer following the classical principles of computation will have certain paradoxical "blind spots." There will be things such a computational system just can't decide on. But we, it's claimed, suffer from no such limitations. How could this be? Well, maybe our brains exploit quantum effects to leap outside classical computational limitations. We may be quantum computers! And it may be that the special features of consciousness, the ones that don't show up in an ordinary physical story, just are the special quantum features allowing us to achieve the special open-ended thinking we can engage in. While it's not clear that such a view is really best characterized as dualist, it fits well with the sorts of views discussed in this section. There is an influence outside those tracked in our classical, deterministic picture. There is an additional element here, one going beyond what ordinary machines can achieve. And there is a distinct role for consciousness beyond the role of classically construed neurons. So I'll locate the view here and leave the question of the best thing to call it for others.[14]

To recap, what do we get from these interactionist views? First, there is the reasonable charge that claims of the causal closure of physics are less secure than it first appeared. Modern science, particularly when faced with the enormous complexity of neural interactions, as well the special things our brains can do, may well be fully open to accepting consciousness as a causal force. It may be that we can find this causal impact in the nonlinear chaotic patterns of brain interaction. Once we get a better picture of such patterns, we may indeed find the causal patterns the dualists seek. Or maybe quantum mechanics positively needs consciousness to stand outside the network of probable patterns to "collapse" things to our ordinary classical world. Or maybe QM is needed to explain what we do mentally. Either way, we need something beyond the usual closed picture of physical causation, the one that seemed so central to our scientific worldview. This apparent centrality is the product of a naive view of science, so there's nothing anti-scientific here. Indeed, naturalistic dualism may seem more in tune with the most current science!

So, what's the problem here? Why not go dualist and accept what our intuitions seem to be saying in the first place? The basic problem comes down to our optimism about explaining consciousness. Interactionist dualism posits consciousness as a new basic feature of reality. Maybe. But the other sorts of things we posit as basic are smaller and more widely distributed than consciousness seems to be, at least at first blush. Gravity and electromagnetism are forces affecting all things at all scales. And quarks, the basic building blocks of physical theory, are tiny, almost beyond measure. These things then combine to make up all the higher-level things we see and to account for all the particular things we observe. Consciousness, on the other hand, doesn't seem like this kind of property. It seems to be a macro- rather than a micro-phenomenon. It happens to us mid-sized featherless bipeds. Odd to think that such a thing is *basic*. It might be, but the history of the success of reductive explanation suggests otherwise. In the past, seemingly irreducible macro-level phenomena have succumbed to reductive explanation in terms of the more universal forces and more tiny particles. This isn't a "knock-down" argument, but it gives one pause.

At root, in my opinion, is the question of just how exceptional, just how different, consciousness is. Is it really the one place we need to revise our reductive picture, to add in new properties to our ontology? There is an "anti-Copernican" vibe here. Copernicus, with his heliocentric view, knocked us out of the central place of creation. And the progress of science since then has been to further this Copernican transformation. It may be depressing, but it seems we are not the main actors on the stage of reality. We are just another collection of matter, no more special than anything else, requiring no special revisions of reality. There is a suspicion that jumping to dualism now, going "pessimistic" on the mystery and adding to our ontology, is motivated, maybe unconsciously, by a desire to put the brakes on the grim march of the Copernicans. But for those of us with a strong Copernican tendency, we shouldn't expect to find such an exceptional property right at the heart of humanity. So even if there's space for a more complex, non-closed causal story, we should be suspicious of it and we should keep looking for physical methods, in the standard sense of normal, macro-level biological causation, to explain our experience.

Wow, what a killjoy! Indeed, this line of thought may serve as a *reductio* of the reductionist. Is that really all they think we are? For my part, I think it's super amazing that we might "just" be a physical system. I find it incredibly inspirational to think of myself and the rest of humanity in this way. But I've always rooted for the robots in science fiction movies. Is there any other problem with the dualist position? One is that it is profoundly unsatisfying as an explanation of consciousness. It doesn't, in fact, explain consciousness at all. It simply says consciousness just is what is, and not another thing, full stop. And then we do our best to connect it to the other elements of our reality. Such a position is not incoherent, nor is it obviously flawed or discredited. But it represents, to me at least, a kind of explanatory surrender, just when things are getting interesting! As an explanatory optimist, I say give us, oh, another thousand years of investigation before we throw in the towel and posit consciousness as a new primitive. It may be that's the best we can do, but we can't know that yet. Or so I would argue. But before we move on to non-dualist views, we need to consider the other branch of dualism, known as epiphenomenalism. Epiphenomenalism accepts the causal closure of physics but holds that conscious properties are distinct from the physical nonetheless.

Epiphenomenal Dualism

Epiphenomenalism accepts the causal closure of the physical world but still maintains that consciousness is nonphysical.[15] This means that consciousness cannot have any causal impact on our world, including on how our bodies behave! Something is epiphenomenal when it stands outside the chain of causation. A famous example is of a steam whistle driven by the excess pressure of a steam locomotive. Steam pressure drives the pistons, producing the movement of the engine. But excess pressure can be routed through a reed, producing the lonesome trilling of a train. But the whistle does not contribute to the moving of the engine – it is epiphenomenal in that sense. It is out of the causal loop. Epiphenomenal dualism holds that consciousness is like that: out of the loop of physical causation. Conscious states may be caused by physical changes in the brain, but conscious states are themselves causally inert. They are a causal dead end.

This view is widely seen as counterintuitive. It's truly weird. It says that the conscious feeling of pain does not cause our screaming or our evasive action. That all occurs because of prior action in the brain. The feeling is just an inert by-product. And the same holds true of our conscious perceptions, conscious desires, and conscious intentions. The conscious mind is just along for the ride with the physical body. And the view also has to accept that our knowledge of our conscious states can't be caused by the conscious states themselves, at least if we think that our knowledge can influence how we act. The view has to reject a causal theory of knowledge for our first-person knowledge of consciousness. Usually, we'd think that our knowledge that we're in pain is caused by the feeling of pain. But this is ruled out on the epiphenomenal view. All this seems like a rather radical move. What can be said in the view's favor?

The epiphenomenalist embraces two ideas (Robinson 2004). One is that there really is no way around the causal closure of the physical. The interactionist's appeal to strange quantum effects or complex, chaotic statistics doesn't change the fact that, when we look at ourselves in terms of our bodily actions, there just doesn't seem to be a place to "slip in" nonphysical causation. Consider my deliberate moving of my fingers while typing this page. We know from physiology that a series of muscle contractions move my fingers. What's more, we know how neurons connected to my muscles act to initiate, coordinate, and control such movements. Indeed, we know right down to the molecular level how these processes work. Or we have a good idea of how they go, and nothing indicates a need to posit any outside influence. And this process can be traced right up through the brain in the same fashion. Further, understanding the behaving body in this way has been extremely fruitful for physiology, medicine, and other applied sciences. To go against causal closure here seems quite clearly to run against the dominant trend in the relevant sciences, the sciences pitched at the right level, where we live. The quantum world is an odd place and, thankfully, it looks like it can be safely ignored at the level of human behavior. Hence, physical causal closure should be respected as one of the more secure pieces of knowledge we have about how the body works.

But epiphenomenalists also take the arguments against the possibility of physicalism to heart. They think that arguments like the zombie show that there just cannot be a workable physicalist theory of consciousness: no further amount of physical theorizing will explain how it is that the feeling of a sharp pain or the visual experience of a tropical sunset is merely a brain process. So, if we are to respect the scientific need for closure *and* the irreducibility of conscious experience, we are left holding that consciousness is a real, distinct existent that does no causal work. We are forced by two well-supported claims into what seems to be an uncomfortable position. But all the views surveyed in this book must embrace *some* weirdness. The philosophical rug always bumps up somewhere, as I've already mentioned. Reductionists have to deny what seems manifest about conscious experience: that it appears more than a mere physical, functional process. And interactionist dualists have to junk causal closure. By saving these two things, maybe the epiphenomenalist is doing the best we can do here!

Further, there may well be interesting empirical evidence suggesting something like epiphenomenalism when it comes to consciousness. Psychologist Daniel Wegner and colleagues produced a range of studies where it seems that our conscious experience of doing something happens *after we've done it*![16] And in other cases, we can be made to feel that we've actively done something when we didn't do it at all. These studies seem to show that consciousness "arrives" too late to affect what our brains have already done and, further, that consciousness is interpretive, meaning that it tries best to interpret what's already occurred, rather than doing anything itself. And there are studies from neuroscience providing further weight to this case. Neuroscientist Benjamin Libet did experiments where subjects were simply required to push a button while judging when they decided to do so (Libet 1985).[17] A reliable result of these studies is that key "action potentials" in the brain signifying the initiation of action occur *almost half a second* before we consciously feel we've initiated the action! To put this another way, our brains kick us into action and consciousness only gets the word half a second later. But we still feel that we caused the button push. It still seems to us that there is no mismatch between our consciously deciding to act and the action. But the results suggest otherwise. They seem to say that the action occurs without consciousness causing it, just as the epiphenomenalist would predict. Now, the proper interpretation of these results is a matter of much scholarly debate and there are other ways to interpret them that do not support full-blown dualist epiphenomenalism. But the fact that there's this sort of debate at all shows that epiphenomenalism may not be as off-track as it seems at first blush.

But the fact remains that epiphenomenal dualism is not a popular view. And this is mainly due to its rejection of a causal role for consciousness. While it may be that consciousness is in less causal control than we thought, it would be just amazing if it had *no* influence on our behavior whatsoever. Perhaps consciousness is merely a veto system, one that can block instinctual or automated action initiated unconsciously. Consciousness may not start things, but it might stop them. But this requires causal influence and can't be allowed by epiphenomenalism. Or perhaps consciousness is less an actor and more of a reporter or storyteller. Maybe most action we engage in leaves consciousness out of the loop, and consciousness comes in later to explain what's going on, to apologize for our errors, or to claim our successes. Or at least to rationalize what we're doing. But again, even in this more limited role, consciousness must be able to cause our verbal reports, our rationalizing and storytelling. Even this small job is ruled out by epiphenomenalism. And finally, if epiphenomenalism is true, it is hard to see how consciousness might have evolved. Evolution selects those things that provide a *behavioral* advantage. Epiphenomenal phenomena can't do that by definition. The best the epiphenomenalist can offer is that consciousness is connected to the brain – it emerges out of complex brain processes, though it, itself, is not physical – and those brain processes *were* selected for. This is not out of the question, but it rules out a class of explanation for consciousness and demands a nice piece of metaphysical luck. Consciousness just happened to be connected to a physical process that was evolutionarily useful; if it wasn't, we wouldn't be conscious. And indeed, it's possible that some beings weren't so lucky: our friends the zombies. At the end of the day, epiphenomenalism has the feel of a "last resort" position, not far from pessimistic mysterianism. There's a one-way connection between the physical brain and consciousness, and that's about all we can say.

To conclude this chapter, we can say that while there may be strong intuitive reasons, provided by zombies and the like, to think that consciousness couldn't be physical, there is substantial cost to dualism as well. First, we have to posit a very non-Copernican addition to our basic ontology – we need to add what seems to be a high-level, complex, and nonuniversal item to our basic list. Second, by doing so, we rule out the possibility of saying anything else informative about the nature of consciousness. It just is what it is, like gravity or Popeye. And third, we must deal with the interaction question, either by rejecting the causal closure of the physical and positing some additional causal element or by rejecting interaction altogether. These difficulties may well be forced on us by the arguments. Zombies are hard to kill! But the difficulties of dualism have inspired many thinkers to craft a rival sort of nonreductive view or to reject zombies and reduce, reduce, reduce. We will survey those attempts in what follows. First up is a class of related nonreductive views, in many ways a close cousin of dualism, which rejects both reduction and a metaphysically expansive dualism. Among these nonreductive views are neutral monism and panpsychism. A true metaphysical menagerie.

Further Reading

See Chalmers (1996 and 2010) for much more on the varieties of dualism. See Penrose's *The Emperor's New Mind: Concerning Computers, Minds, and the Laws of Physics* for an introduction to his view. And for a well worked-out defense of epiphenomenalism, see William Robinson's *Understanding Phenomenal Consciousness*. For a collection on contemporary dualism (and other issues addressed in this book), see Shear (ed.), *Explaining Consciousness: The Hard Problem*.

4
Nonreductive Views

So far, it looks like there are two big competing views about the nature of consciousness. The first, physicalism, holds that consciousness (and everything else) is ultimately just something physical. The other, dualism, holds that there are two basic kinds of stuff in the world: physical stuff and phenomenal (or conscious) stuff.[1] Either it's all physical or we have to add something to our basic ontology, the philosopher's official and complete catalog of what there is. But a number of philosophers have tried to find a middle way between these two views, a position acknowledging the irreducibility of consciousness to the physical, but still rejecting out-and-out dualism. Is there really any space for such a view? Can we really hold consciousness separate but keep it from "flying off" on its own? And if we don't endorse full-blown dualism, what's to keep consciousness from reducing back into the underlying physical stuff? Views trying to walk this thin line are called "nonreductive" in this book because I am reserving the term "reduction" for *physical* reduction. Obviously, dualism is nonreductive as well, so we can call the array of views we'll look at in this chapter "nonreductive, non-dualistic" views, though I'll just call them "nonreductive" for short.[2]

So, how do we arrive at a nonreductive view? First, remember what the zombie argument purportedly shows. We can conceive of a being physically just like us but lacking consciousness. But what does it mean to say that the being is physically just like us? It means that everything that physics says about us, it also says about our zombie twin. But when we dig a bit deeper about just what physics tells us about the world, we find a surprising gap. Theories in physics deal in what we can call "relational" information only. Relational information tells us how things are lawfully connected, how changing one thing changes another according to the physical laws posited by the theory. And then, in turn, we can define physical things like electrons, protons, or quarks in terms of how they fit into this framework of causal connections. As noted in the last chapter, on this view to be an electron is just to be the kind of thing that fits into this pattern of causal relations – that plays this "causal role." We learn with extreme precision from physical theory just what this special electron "role" is. But we don't learn, so it seems, just what the thing playing the role is, on its own. It's like learning all we can about what it is to be a goalie: a goalie is the person who defends the goal and can use his or her hands to stop the ball, who can't touch the ball when it's passed back by his or her own team, who usually kicks the goal kicks, and so on, without learning *who is playing goalie for our team*. We know all about the goalie role without learning that its Hope Solo or Tim Howard. We learn the role without learning about the role-filler, beyond that he or she plays that role. But there may be other things true of the role-filler beyond what he or she does in the role.

This point about what physics tells us was made most famously by the British philosopher Bertrand Russell. Russell writes: "The physical world is only known as regards certain abstract features of its space–time structure – features which, because of their abstractness, do not suffice to show whether the physical world is, or is not, different in intrinsic character from the world of mind" (1992 [1948]: 240). Because the language of physics is highly mathematical, the best we can get out of physics is an extremely abstract characterization of things in terms of lawful causes and effects. We don't learn about the "intrinsic character" of physical things – what they are like in and of themselves, disconnected from the causal patterns they figure in. For all we know, according to Russell, the role-player of physical stuff might be something mental, something phenomenal, to use our current terminology. The inner core of physical stuff is left undescribed by physics. We get all the relations without the "relata." And this opens up the space for a nonreductive answer to the zombie.

Rather than saying that the zombie shows consciousness is nonphysical, it might be that the zombie shows that consciousness is the product of (or is instantiated by) the intrinsic core left out of our physical theory. Zombies have something playing the same roles as our physical stuff, but the zombie's role-players have a different "intrinsic character" from ours. The things playing the role in us are phenomenal, or are the sorts of things that could generate conscious experience when clumped together in the right way. In zombies, the role-fillers lack this phenomenal element. Their physical roles are realized by cold, dark, non-phenomenal role-fillers. It might seem that this is a kind of dualism: we've got role-fillers with special nonphysical features. But proponents of these nonreductive views deny the real metaphysical separation indicative of dualism. Some hold that it's best to see whatever it is that fills the gap in our physics as *physical* – after all, it's playing physical roles. Or perhaps there is something basic and phenomenal filling the role, but it's an aspect of all physical matter. This may seem very close to dualism, but it puts the irreducible bit at the foundation of *everything*. This sort of view is known as "panpsychism." Or maybe what's filling the key roles is something "neutral," a third sort of stuff, neither physical nor phenomenal, out of which both the physical and phenomenal emerge. This view is called "neutral monism." In what follows, I'll lay out the various nonreductive approaches trying to squeeze through what we can call "Russell's gap." This is a space of complex metaphysics and subtle philosophical differences, so we'll try to tread carefully. One problem in this area is figuring out how views really differ. And a major objection to the general approach is that it collapses back into physicalism or dualism, despite the best intentions of its developers. But hard problems may require hard solutions. There's no free philosophical lunch, alas.

Russell's Gap and Physical Theory

What Russell's gap shows us is that there's something left out of our most complete physical story about the world – namely, the intrinsic nature of physical stuff. Another way to put this is that all physics tells us about is what physical stuff is *disposed to do*: what physical law dictates will occur, given certain antecedent conditions. In philosophers' terms, physics only tells us about the *dispositional properties* of physical stuff, not the *categorical base* of these dispositions. A paradigm dispositional property is *fragility*. Something is fragile if it is disposed to break in certain situations. When we learn that a window is fragile, we learn that it will likely break if hit even softly. But there is a further question we can ask about the window or any fragile object. What is it about the makeup of the window that gives it this dispositional property? The answer is that the window has a certain molecular structure with bonds that are relatively weak in key areas. This molecular structure is what we call the *categorical base* for the window's fragility. Returning to physics, at its most basic level, all we get is the dispositional properties, not the categorical base. We learn that electrons (or quarks or "hadrons") are things disposed to do such-and-such, to be repelled by certain charges, to move in certain ways. We don't learn what's "underneath" making this happen.

Now for the key nonreductive maneuver. Nonreductionists contend that, whatever the categorical base of physical stuff is, for all we know it may be phenomenal. This isn't ruled out by the physics. What's more, because we can't learn any more from physics about the stuff in question – physics "bottoms out" at dispositional properties – there is no conflict with the physical sciences. Claiming that the categorical base of physical stuff is phenomenal doesn't mess with physics *at all* – so long as the dispositions remain the same, physics runs smoothly. So this sort of nonreductive view is fully consistent with science. What's more, there is no worry, at least at the outset, of epiphenomenalism. The intrinsic categorical base is needed to fill the causal roles of physical stuff. It's what does the real causal work, presumably. So whenever we have behavior, there will be some phenomenal stuff involved, because the causal basis for the behavioral dispositions *is phenomenal*. We thus get a view that is fully compatible with the findings of science but holds a place for experience. And experience doesn't get shut out of the causal process, as it's in danger of doing with dualism. Rather, it plays the key role in making our behavior happen.

So there seem to be clear benefits to the nonreductive view. But now we must dig in to the details of how various proposals fill in Russell's gap with the stuff of consciousness. There are several ways to go. One is to say that there is a basic and irreducible phenomenal element at the heart of all physical matter. It is basic and it is everywhere. This view is called *panpsychism*: everywhere that there is matter, there is a little bit of consciousness as well. Alternately, one could deny that there is phenomenality *everywhere* that there is matter and say, rather, that there is the special ingredient for phenomenality everywhere there is matter. When the right clumping of this "proto-phenomenality" is present, we get full-blown consciousness, but not before. This has the advantage of avoiding the need to say that every bit of matter, from rocks to radios, is conscious. But it must explain what this proto-phenomenality is and how it brings consciousness into being. David Chalmers has labeled this view with the catchy name of *panprotopsychism*. Another way to go is to say there is something more basic than either physical matter or consciousness, out of which both are made. This more basic stuff is said to be neutral between conscious mind and physical matter and provides the reductive base for both. The neutral stuff stands as the categorical base for physical dispositions, but it also, in the right circumstances, instantiates the intrinsic character of conscious experience as well. The view is called *neutral monism* and it was (at some points) the view of Russell himself.

We can ask of a nonreductive view if it is "basic" or "emergent" when it comes to consciousness.[3] Basic views hold that consciousness can't be explained by or reduced to anything else. Emergent views hold that consciousness emerges out of something more basic. Note that physicalism as it's standardly construed is an emergent view. Consciousness emerges from more basic physical matter on the standard picture. On nonreductive emergent views, consciousness does not emerge from physical stuff, but from a proto-phenomenal or neutral monistic base, so they are able to avoid the problem of showing how consciousness could possibly emerge from stuff described solely in physical terms. But they have the burden of showing how their alternative picture works! Basic nonreductive views, by contrast, don't have the problem of explaining how consciousness emerges from anything more basic. But they have to deal with the ubiquity of consciousness – of "global" panpsychism.

So we have basic and emergent nonreductive views: views that make consciousness explanatorily basic and views that have some more basic neutral stuff (or events, or whatever . . . see below!) at the bottom level of reality. The theories discussed in this chapter actually have quite a rich history, from the panpsychism of Spinoza and Leibniz in the early modern period to the neutral monism of William James and Bertrand Russell in the early part of the twentieth century.[4] These older versions are well developed and complex but, given the focus of this book, we'll stick to current versions of the views. One version of modern-day panpsychism is Galen Strawson's "realistic monism." Strawson sees it as version of physicalism, but he acknowledges that most see it as a nonreductive view. We'll focus on Strawson's position first, as it represents a clear version of a basic, nonemergent panpsychism, one that relies on Russell's gap to find space for phenomenal properties. We'll then look at Daniel Stoljar's nonreductive view, again one labeled by its author as a version of physicalism, though it clearly fits into our nonreductive slot. Then we consider Chalmers's panprotopsychism, and follow it with some reflections on neutral monism. We'll close the chapter by noting difficulties these views face.[5]

Strawson's Realistic Monism

Galen Strawson argues for what he calls "realistic monism" (Strawson 1994, 2006). There are two main ideas motivating Strawson's position. One is the claim that there's basically just one kind of fundamental stuff. Philosophers label this kind of view "monism." The other is the seemingly utterly obvious claim that experiences are real. But Strawson argues that if you take both of these claims seriously, you end up with a version of panpsychism. This conclusion is surprising, Strawson argues, because most philosophers have been wildly confused about what it means to hold that experiences are real. First and foremost, claims Strawson, this rules out *any* kind of reduction of experience to the usual kind of functional-physical stuff. The usual functional-physical stuff is so utterly different from experience that any attempt to reduce experience to it amounts to *eliminativism*: the elimination of experience from our ontology. And this is truly an absurd thing to do. It's to claim that we only seem to be conscious, but we are not. But if it "seems" any way to us at all, surely that entails we're conscious! So it seems hard to state the eliminativist view even coherently. And yet, Strawson notes, many contemporary philosophers take this path. They hold views that, when looked at carefully, entail the elimination of consciousness altogether! Strawson stresses that, viewed from a bit of distance, this is amazingly nutty, but philosophers are famous throughout history for embracing some pretty wild ideas.[6]

So how are we to avoid the absurdity of eliminativism? Most philosophers, in opposition to Strawson, contend that consciousness emerges out of something more basic. It's not that there is no consciousness; rather, it's that consciousness just is made up of something more fundamental. But here Strawson challenges all attempts at laying out an emergent picture. For emergence to make any sense at all – for it to avoid being just a blind leap of faith – there must be some kind of reasonable connection between the underlying stuff and the emergent phenomenal features. We can see this with other examples of emergent phenomena. Liquidity, for example, emerges from the arrangement of molecules because we can see how the nature of certain molecular bonds makes something liquid rather than solid or gaseous. Likewise, we can see how the right organization and functioning of certain chemical processes could instantiate life. But we have exactly *no* idea of how any organization of molecules or atoms or quarks or whatever could instantiate an experience of blue or the feeling of a paper cut. These categories seem completely disparate and distinct. So we have no idea at all how consciousness could be an emergent phenomenon.

Someone might argue that philosophers and scientists of the past had the same intuitions about life and liquidity. Maybe we're just under the temporary ignorance of the moderate mysterian? But Strawson reiterates the fundamental difference between consciousness and these other cases, writing

> This very tired objection is always made in discussions of this sort, and the first thing to note is that one cannot draw a parallel between the perceived problem of life and the perceived problem of experience in this way, arguing that the second problem will dissolve just as the first did, unless one considers life completely apart from experience. So let us call life considered completely apart from experience 'life*'. My reply is then brief. Life* reduces, experience doesn't . . . We can explain its life* functions in exquisite detail in the terms of current sciences of physics, chemistry and biology. We cannot explain its experience at all in these terms. (2006: 20)

If we cannot reduce and elimination is absurd, then we must accept experience as basic. So far, we are walking the same path as the dualist. But now the first consideration kicks in: there is ultimately just one kind of stuff. Why think this?

There are two main reasons to adopt monism over dualism. First, it avoids dualism's problems with causal interaction. If there's just one stuff, then we don't have to worry about a distinct and fundamentally different sort of thing getting into contact with and manipulating the physical body. It's all just one stuff and both consciousness and the brain are constituted by it. So when I consciously desire ice cream and I find myself in front of the fridge for that reason, the conscious desire can be the cause of my behavior because the physical stuff doing the causing is itself conscious. And secondly, there is no conflict here with the findings of the natural sciences. The realistic monist can accept all that science has to offer and still hold a place for real experience. One way to put this is that the realistic monist holds that the physical sciences do not tell us everything about physical matter. And, because of this, there is room to locate the irreducible phenomenal properties of consciousness at the heart of physical matter itself. Strawson maintains that this really is the best way to have a satisfying version of physicalism. We shouldn't be restricted by the language of physics in what we think about the under-lying nature of physical stuff. And given that we know – better than we know anything else! – that we are indeed conscious and having experiences, it makes sense to hold that the aspects of physical matter left untouched by the physical science are themselves fundamentally phenomenal.

Whether or not this is a substantial improvement over physicalism and dualism is a question we'll take up at the end of the chapter. For now, though, note that we're left with a view that is nonemergent – it holds that the phenom-enal features of reality can't be reduced to anything non-phenomenal. But does it then follow that everything in nature, from humans to hockey pucks to hot springs, is really con-scious? What could this mean? Strawson mentions this doesn't *necessarily* follow from his view. One could hold that only *some* bits of matter have a phenomenal aspect and that those may be lacking from the underlying matter making up hockey pucks and hot springs. On such a view, there is more than one type of "ultimate", the basic constituents of reality. One type has a phenomenal aspect, the other does not. And, perhaps, those bits with a phenomenal core are only found in the brains of sentient, complex creatures. If that were the case, then we wouldn't have to embrace full-blown panpsy-chism, where *everything* is at least a little bit conscious. But Strawson rejects this position. He points out that it seems completely ad hoc – why are only some bits of matter, and just the ones we intuitively want, the ones with bits of phe-nomenality? What's more, this really now does seem *very* close to dualism: when we have complex brains, then a special nonphysical property is present, instantiating our conscious experiences. Still, this may offer some hope of avoiding the problem of epiphenomenalism, as the phenomenal features fill "Russell's gap" in the physical elements of our brains.

In any event, Strawson embraces full-blown panpsychism, where everything really does have a bit of consciousness accompanying it. Sure, this is odd, but given the seeming impossibility of reduction and the worries about conscious causation, such a position may be forced on us. And we needn't think that the consciousness of a hockey puck or a hot spring is just like our consciousness! Sure, there must be *something* it's like for those things, in a minimal sense, but it needn't be that hockey pucks sit dreading the slap shot and hoping for smooth, clean ice. What exactly it is like for them may remain beyond our knowledge, but that does not mean we have to posit our sort of conscious mental life. And, finally, all views in this area are going to have to say something weird, one would think. The weirdness pops up somewhere and maybe the right place to put it is where the panpsychic does: everywhere. At least they don't have to deny the complex reality of causally efficacious consciousness and the findings of modern physical science.

Stoljar's Ignorance Hypothesis and Chalmers's Panprotopsychism

But perhaps the nonreductionist needn't stick his explanatory neck out quite so far. Philosopher Daniel Stoljar follows Strawson and other nonreductionists in taking Russell's gap as the starting point for addressing the problem of consciousness, but he remains deliberately noncommittal about just what fills the gap (Stoljar 2001, 2006). So long as it is something that realizes conscious experience as well as the dispositional bases of physical matter, that is enough to avoid the zombie argument. And that leaves physicalism (of a sort) still standing, saving our general scientific worldview and the reality of conscious experience. Stoljar notes that we can distinguish two kinds of physical truths: those that physical theory tells us about and those concerning the categorical, intrinsic nature of physical objects. The properties picked out by physical theory Stoljar calls "t-physical properties" and the categorical, intrinsic properties of physical objects – those missed by physics – he calls "o-physical properties." The zombie argument trades on the fact that physical facts don't seem to entail facts about phenomenal consciousness. We can't tell by "reading off" the physical facts what the phenomenal facts are. But the argument only touches on t-physical properties. If, somehow, we had in our hands the facts about o-physical properties, we might well be able to determine what the phenomenal facts amount to. And so we might be able to rule out zombies. Because the zombie argument does not block this possibility, it is logically flawed: there is a space left open for a nonreductive view appealing to o-physical properties. And that is what Stoljar proposes.

But what *are* o-physical properties? About these, the less said, the better. All we need here is a way to block the zombie. And our ignorance of o-physical properties does just that. We can't be expected to rule out (or rule in!) zombies if we don't know all the physical facts. And that's just what is demanded by the zombie argument. We're told that, given *all* the physical facts, zombies are possible. But we do not possess at present all the physical facts, given our ignorance of o-physical properties. So we're off the zombie hook. Now, we could take a few more steps and follow Strawson down the road to panpsychism. But there's no need if all we want is a stalemate with the zombie hordes. Panpsychism is certainly consistent with Stoljar's view (as is a worked-out version of panproto-psychism or neutral monism). But given the weirdness of those views, perhaps silence (or modesty) is the way to go here. It may be less than satisfying to stop here but, in the back-and-forth of the argument, we may at least be able to block a move to all-out dualism.

And what about Chalmers in all this, the king of the zombies? Chalmers himself makes clear that the zombie argument does *not* entail dualism, only the falseness of the more standard reductive versions of physicalism (the views we'll take up in the later chapters of this book). What he calls "type-F monism" is consistent with the zombie argument, as well as the "naturalistic dualism" discussed in the previous chapter. Type-F monism is a version of the sort of nonreductive view we're looking at here. Chalmers describes several ways of fleshing out type-F monism (Chalmers 1996; 2010: chs 1 and 5; 2013). One is the sort of panpsychism endorsed by Strawson, but another rejects the idea that all fundamental features of reality must be conscious. Rather, they might be made of the sort of thing that, when combined in the right way, generates consciousness. These "proto-phenomenal" properties have an intrinsic nature producing phenomenal experience, but they themselves are not conscious. There is thus no need to accept that all matter is conscious. Proto-phenomenal properties are not describable in terms of physical theory. Again, they are the underlying categorical bases of physical stuff, the intrinsic core left out in Russell's gap. And, again, because they also fill the categorical role in physical causation, there is no worry about epiphenomenalism. But what is the nature of this proto-phenomenal material? It's not captured in physical theory, due to Russell's gap. But it's not phenomenal by definition, so we can't unpack it in terms of "what it's like" for a subject. It lies at a blind spot of our theorizing. But this is not the end of the world. As we keep seeing in this chapter, it's hard to do metaphysics. We keep having to talk about things that there seems to be no good way to talk about! Following Stoljar, we may embrace this metaphysical ignorance as a virtue, using it to keep zombies at bay. Or perhaps an as-of-yet unimagined sort of theorizing might shed at least a *little* light on the nature of proto-phenomenal properties. A temporary mysterianism here is an option. And, of course, we just may never know. Such may be the sad lot of us mere mortals, alas. But there is nothing seriously off with this metaphysical position. And though I just said that metaphysics is hard, maybe it's actually extremely easy. Just say anything that's not an out-and-out logical contradiction, and you're doing fine!

Neutral Monism

Chalmers's panprotopsychism brings us very close to an older version of the nonreductive approach, so-called "neutral monism." In the latter part of the nineteenth century and the early part of the twentieth, a number of eminent philosophers and scientists embraced versions of this view. The idea, having its roots in the work of David Hume, is that we should do away with any talk of *substances*.[7] There is no underlying physical substrata and no underlying mental "ego" to which all the mental happenings occur. All we need to posit are a series of "happenings" or "events." And these events, taken in and of themselves, are neither physical nor mental. They are neutral. But, in some contexts, an event can be seen as a mental event and, in other contexts, the same event can be taken as physical. The idea is *not* that events are whatever we take them to be – that sort of subjective construction is out. Rather, there are real events with subject-independent features that are mental in some contexts and physical in others. A perception of a blue sphere is both a physical event – there is something involving objects and light and neural reactions – and a mental event: there is a bluish perception occurring. There is no underlying ego or self to which the event appears, so we don't need to deal with that kind of mental thing. There's just neutral "happenings" in one context or another.

The view was developed in the nineteenth century by Ernst Mach and then William James, before being taken up by Russell in the 1920s. The basic happenings are said to be neutral, meaning that they are neither fundamentally physical nor mental. They are not physical because Russell took his gap to show that physics just doesn't say enough about objects to tell us about their real nature. And they are not mental because, so it was argued, they could in principle exist without anyone perceiving, thinking, or being aware of them. They are *mind-independent* things. These neutral events provide the underlying "reductive" base for both physical and mental things. For Russell, physical and mental things are constructed out of the neutral base. So we arrive at a view close to Chalmers's panprotopsychism, but with a few differences. For one, there is no need to say that proto-phenomenal properties are fundamental and ubiquitous. Rather, when the right conditions occur, then we get phenomenality. So we get an emergent view, one on which something non-phenomenal generates the phenomenal in certain situations. It may be that this is what Chalmers intends by "proto-phenomenal," but it may be that the neutrality of the older view is stronger, rejecting even the "proto-mental" from the neutral base.

We can see that the neutral monist can say many of the same things about zombies as those defending the other views canvassed here. But their other metaphysical commitments – the rejection of underlying substances, both physical and mental – create some interesting issues beyond the scope of our discussion.[8] We are *deep* in the metaphysical ocean now, so perhaps we should try to get back to some solid ground. But before we leave the nonreductivists, we'll consider some of the general worries about the approach, some that we've briefly touched on already and one big issue we've yet to discuss.

Worries About Nonreductive Views

The first worry about the nonreductive approach is that it slides back into either dualism or more traditional versions of physicalism. Dualism says that phenomenal properties are not reducible to any physical property and concludes that they must be something metaphysically distinct. But because most modern-day dualists are *property* dualists (see ch. 3: 37–9), they don't think that phenomenal properties exist on their own. Indeed, they are nonphysical properties of *brains*. So they are glued very tightly, in a metaphysical sense, to certain bits of physical matter. The nonreductivists surveyed in this chapter, particularly those who hold that phenomenal properties are emergent out of some neutral or proto-phenomenal base, hold that when you've got matter arranged as a brain, full-fledged phenomenal properties emerge. Now, the proto-phenomenal properties are already present in the matter, but they haven't "transformed" yet. But one might think that a dualist's phenomenal properties are emergent from the underlying materials as well. Where were they, after all, before they glommed on to a brain? So there seems to be little real difference between the views. And certainly in spirit, the nonreductionist and the dualist are fellow travelers. First and foremost, they reject a physicalist reduction of consciousness. And that means they are not looking to the physical sciences to settle the issue about what consciousness amounts to. There is a difference, however, in how the *causal* issue is handled. The dualist must either accept epiphenomenalism or reject the causal closure of the physical. By locating phenomenal properties as categorical bases of physical things, the nonreductionist avoids this worry. But the cost is either panpsychism or the positing of seemingly unknowable proto-phenomenal properties, neither physical nor phenomenal in nature.

What's more, it's not clear that there's a smooth path from the properties needed to fill Russell's gap in physics to

phenomenal properties. The reasoning to phenomenal properties goes something like this: Look, we need something
intrinsic to fill the causal roles in physics. And consciousness
has an intrinsic nature we know in experience. So phenomenal properties, being intrinsic, can be the intrinsic role-fillers
in physics. But there is an ambiguity in the use of "intrinsic"
here. We've got two ideas at play. One is what we might call
"causal intrinsic": whatever it is that stands as the categorical base for physical dispositions. This is given to us by Russell's gap. But, in experience, we are in contact with what we
can call "phenomenal intrinsic," a quality like the reddishness of a visual experience. We know the quality in an intimate way. But we don't in this way get any inkling about
how such a property could do *any causing,* especially in the
sense given by Russell's gap. What is it about reddishness or
the salty taste of pork rinds that suggests that those sorts of
properties could explain or instantiate or have anything to
do with the causal interactions of massive bodies or subatomic particles or what have you? The two sorts of intrinsics are so different as to defy any informative connection at
all, beyond the fact that they stand at the foundation of their
respective theories. To simply move from one to the other
and call it a day is a rather quick step! But perhaps there just
doesn't need to be any explanation of how the two sorts of
intrinsics fit together. So long as it's not ruled out by the
physics, we can slot in the phenomenal and see what follows.
But if one were hoping for a bit more explanatory kick, it is
sadly lacking. And this again highlights the closeness, in
spirit if not in letter, of dualism and the nonreductive views
looked at here.

And there is also a worry from the other direction,
that what we get in the nonreductive "theory" is nothing
more than we get from the traditional physical reductionist.
This is especially clear with the emergent versions of the
view. Emergent nonreductivists hold that something proto-
phenomenal or neutral generates (or realizes or instantiates
or constitutes . . . note the philosopher's words!) consciousness. But some physical reductionists whom we'll meet in the
next chapter hold a very similar view. They argue that phenomenal properties *just are* physical properties (of the kind
described in physics). But we have no explanation of why this

is so, beyond the co-occurrence of consciousness and certain physical features. And that's OK! We don't get illuminating explanations of everything. What these "weakly reductive" physicalists say is that when you have ("normal") physical stuff laid out brain-wise, you get consciousness. And consciousness is causally efficacious because it *just is* that physical stuff. And our explanation bottoms out here. But now we can ask if this is substantially different from the emergent nonreductive position. Both hold that when you put physical matter together brain-wise, you get experience. And both hold that experience is causally efficacious. They just differ on exactly how they tie the phenomenal to the physical. One sees it as the underlying categorical base. The other sees it as identical to some physical properties or processes or what have you. Neither offers a more in-depth explanation of why these bits of physical matter consciously feel this way or that. And, what's more, both seem equally open to Strawson's worry about having to motivate the claim that something phenomenal emerges out of something non-phenomenal. Maybe this can be done, but it seems that the emergent non-reductivist has no advantage over the physicalist invoking a nonexplanatory identity theory (see the next chapter for more on this kind of view).

The basic, nonemergent panpsychism – Galen Strawson's view, say – might be looking pretty good about now. Most of my charges seem to target emergent versions of the view. But there is still an outstanding problem for all these nonreductive views. All hold that whatever consciousness is present in simple bits of physical matter – hockey pucks, hot springs, and the like – it is not as rich and complex as our consciousness. But that leaves a deep theoretical question. How do the simpler bits of phenomenal (or proto-phenomenal) stuff *combine* to form the sorts of things we experience? Philosopher William Seager calls this the "combination problem" for panpsychism and it looks like a serious internal worry (Seager 1999: ch. 9). If each little bit of matter has its own phenomenal element, what principle can explain how these things come together (when arranged brain-wise) and form the seemingly unified and single experience of an individual? This problem almost brings us back full circle to the problem of explaining how physical matter generates consciousness. There may be a bit of progress – at least we have "proto-phenomenal" building blocks, rather than ones specified in dispositional physical terms. But this looks a substantial issue nonetheless. Some nonreductivists try to avoid the combination problem by holding that the phenomenal only emerges at high levels: when we have full-fledged brainy stuff going on. And it emerges complete and unified, rather than disjointed. But this now looks indistinguishable from dualism and inherits serious questions about the causal efficacy of such emergent features. We lose the role-filling element used to deal with Russell's gap. And so the advantage over dualism from that direction is lost.

But all these worries may be surmountable. And perhaps we should expect a metaphysical solution as rich and challenging as this, given the difficulty of the problem of consciousness. But the feeling remains (especially for those of us with a taste for more sparse metaphysical landscapes!) that we've spiraled off the road of understanding here. Perhaps we've been too quick to dismiss the possibility of a proper physicalist solution to the puzzle. Maybe we'll gain insight from actually studying the brain, rather than just musing about zombies and possible worlds. Or maybe the problem itself has been ill-posed and we've been led down the garden path by philosophical confusion. Or, at the very least, it's worth making very sure we haven't, given the tangled metaphysical thickets of the anti-reductionists. In what follows, we'll consider a variety of proposals for a physicalist reduction of consciousness, starting with the "weakly" reductive identity theory and then turning to more bold (and perhaps outrageous) "strongly" reductive approaches.

Further Reading

Two useful entry points for this material are Leopold Stubenberg's article on neutral monism and William Seager and Sean Allen-Hermanson's article on panpsychism, both in the *Stanford Encyclopedia of Philosophy* (SEP). The SEP is an amazingly valuable online resource and it's worth consulting on all the topics we'll consider in this book. See also *Consciousness and its Place in Nature*, edited by Anthony Freeman, a collection with Galen Strawson's "Realistic Monism: Why Physicalism Entails Panpsychism" as the target and commentaries by seventeen top philosophers, including many mentioned in this book. And see Banks (2010).

5
The Identity Theory

The metaphysical complexities of the last chapter may inspire a longing for simplicity, for a return to the simple things in life. And the first reductive view we'll consider, the identity theory, offers just that. The basic claim of the identity theory is that all mental states, conscious states included, are just brain states and nothing more. There are just brains and their physical states and properties, and that's it, metaphysically speaking. Some of these states are conscious states, some aren't. But the conscious states aren't brain states plus some nonphysical conscious add-on, nor are they brain states realized by little globs of consciousness. They're just brain states as they're described by neuroscience. Who'd a thunk it?

The identity theory in its current form can be traced back to the work of philosopher J. J. C. Smart in the late 1950s.[1] At that time in philosophy, many thought it was just *obvious* that the mind and brain were not identical because one could know about and talk meaningfully about the mind without even knowing one had a brain in one's head. But Smart argued that this was much too quick (Smart 1959). The identity theory is not about word meanings per se, but about things in the world. Further, there are good examples of just the sort of identity in science, identity claims where it's clear that the meaning of the terms are not identical, but the identities are true nonetheless. Smart focused on the claim that lightning = an electromagnetic discharge. One could know lots about lightning and even speak intelligently about it without even knowing that electromagnetic phenomena exist. Indeed, prior to Franklin and his kite, that's all anyone ever did. But it is still true that lightning just is electromagnetic discharge (as Franklin in effect showed). So worries about the meanings of the terms must not be relevant here.

Smart went on to argue that all our evidence about the human body and the natural world point to the idea that everything we do, including thinking and feeling, is a result of our biochemical makeup. We may require a very, very complex "wiring diagram" to get the full picture, but that's all we'll need, not wiring plus something additional. Smart contends that the reason to accept this sort of identity claim is *simplicity*. We start out with what seem to be two distinct things, lightning and an electromagnetic discharge, say. We find that whenever we have one, we have the other, in all cases we've considered. Now, it's *logically* possible that we've got two incredibly well-synchronized phenomena that, so far, have always occurred together. Given that we're here engaged in *inductive* reasoning, from a finite set of particular cases to a universal generalization, we could always be wrong in this way. But in the end, it is just a simpler picture of the world to say there's just one thing here. And this justifies our identity claim. What's more, we may get useful new insights by seeing the world in this way. We can apply electromagnetic theory to cases of lightning and see what new things we find. If we have fruitful results over time, that also supports the claim of identity. And that's about it. No logical deductions with a priori premises, no transcendental leaps to the outer reaches of metaphysics. Keep it simple, silly.

But is this really enough to hold off the zombies? And can this really provide a satisfying *explanation* of consciousness? Or is it just a brute, inexplicable fact that certain brain states are conscious states, and that's it? We'll take up these worries (and others) at the end of the chapter. First, we'll turn to a more current version of the identity theory, defended by philosopher Ned Block. We'll also touch on the "new wave" of neural identity theory, defended by William Bechtel and John Bickle and others. Interestingly, identity theorists need not agree about how much of an explanation the identity claim provides. Some are more optimistic about the prospects of explanation than others, as we'll see. But all of them hold that conscious states are just brain states and nothing more.[2]

Block's Distinction Between "Access" and "Phenomenal" Consciousness

Ned Block is an identity theorist when it comes to consciousness. But though he thinks consciousness is nothing but brain activity, he agrees with Chalmers and other anti-reductionists that consciousness cannot be reductively explained in *functional* terms. Indeed, Block famously accuses those with overly optimistic reductive tendencies of being caught up in a confusion, a confusion over an alleged function of consciousness (Block 1995). The concept of consciousness, Block contends, is a "mongrel concept," one covering a number of distinct phenomena. If we are to avoid theoretical misunderstanding, we must carefully distinguish between the various kinds of consciousness. Block focuses on two kinds of consciousness in particular. One he calls "access consciousness," or a-consciousness for short. A-consciousness occurs when a mental state is available in the right way to the rest of the mind. An a-conscious state is poised for use in reasoning and in the rational control of action and speech. If a state plays this sort of functional role – if it stands in the right sort of causal–dispositional relationships – then the state is a-conscious. Thus, a-consciousness is a strictly functional notion. But it is a mistake to think this is the only kind of consciousness, or even the kind of consciousness most of interest in philosophy and science. Another sort of consciousness, which Block labels "phenomenal consciousness," or p-consciousness, is really the central focus of the enduring problem of consciousness. We've already met this term and I've used it throughout to pick out the kind of consciousness allegedly causing all the trouble. P-consciousness is defined not by what it does, by what functional role it plays, but rather by how it "feels" to the conscious subject, by "what it is like" for that subject.[3] Paradigm cases of p-conscious states are pains and perceptual sensations. When we're in pain or when we consciously perceive a sunset or a Miles

Davis trumpet solo, there is something it's like to be us, *for* us. Importantly, Bock argues that p-consciousness is distinct from a-consciousness. In principle, they can be dissociated. And, because of this, many reductionist theories of consciousness miss the point. They claim to explain p-consciousness when they only explain a-consciousness. They are confused.

But why think the two notions are really distinct in the way Block claims? For one, Block notes that we can at least conceive of the difference. Nothing in the functional notion of a-consciousness entails the presence of p-consciousness. And, what's more, there may be real examples of the two coming apart. There is a neurological condition known as "blindsight," where subjects suffer damage to the visual part of their brains but still retain the ability to use visual information.[4] People with blindsight have holes or "scotoma" in their visual fields. When researchers project images onto that portion of their visual field, blindsight subjects deny seeing anything. However, if they are asked to *guess* what is present, for a range of stimuli they are well above chance at getting it right! They say they can't see anything (and we have no reason to doubt them here) but they can clearly pick up all sorts of visual information. So, is this a case of a-consciousness without p-consciousness, a case where the subjects have access to the information carried by a mental state even though there's nothing it's like for them to have the access? Not quite. Unless they are prompted by experimenters, blindsighters can't *do anything* with the information. They don't in fact seem to have the access needed for a-consciousness. But Block argues we can easily imagine "super blindsighters" who have learned to spontaneously guess on their own. They might become so good at this that we can't tell the difference (from the outside) between them and normally sighted subjects. In *that* case, we'd have a-consciousness without p-consciousness. Block further presents a case where pilots who had dental surgery under general anesthetic later, while flying, felt stabbing pains in their jaws just where the surgically affected areas were. Block claims this shows the pilots had phenomenally conscious states – pains – when they were under the general anesthetic, but could not access them. Now, at altitude and without the general anesthetic, the pains recur and are fully accessible. So we can say that the pains in the past were present but unaccessed. But this doesn't quite get there, either. Block's opponents can say that there are unconscious pains (if that makes sense) in the pilot case, and these pains become conscious for the first time when they are accessed in flight. More recently, Block has offered an empirically driven defense of the distinction, citing perception and memory experiments. We'll take that up at the end of the chapter. For now, I hope it's clear enough what Block intends: there is functional notion of consciousness and a phenomenal, "what it's like" notion, and confusing the two leads to trouble. With this distinction in hand, Block argues against strongly reductive functionalist views. And he then argues in favor of his weakly reductive identity theory by employing Smart's simplicity line against the nonreductivists and dualists.

Block's Identity Theory

If a-consciousness and p-consciousness are really distinct, it's pretty easy to see why we can't explain p-consciousness in functional terms. As Block lays it out, p-consciousness is a fully nonfunctional notion. He writes "I take p-conscious properties to be distinct from any cognitive, intentional, or functional property" (1995: 230). Indeed, the "confusion" many allegedly have about consciousness turns on thinking that p-consciousness can be captured in a functionalist theory. A functionalist theory defines consciousness in terms of something playing the right functional role, of something "doing the right thing." We'll take up functionalist theories in the next chapter. Block contends that functionalist theories of consciousness are engaged in a game of "bait and switch" – they bait you with p-consciousness but switch to a functional notion of a-consciousness once they've got you hooked! If Block is correct in his characterization of p-consciousness, it does seem that functionalist theories are non-starters. Defenders of such theories are well aware of Block's challenge and try various ways to show that p-consciousness is functionally characterizable after all. But if we take Block's account as given, functionalism for p-consciousness doesn't seem to be an option.

But if we can't give a functional characterization of p-consciousness, then aren't we well on the way to a nonreductive or dualist position? Arguably, the main route to reducing complex, high-level things to more basic physical things is by way of functional reduction. Functional reduction, to rehash, first defines a thing in terms of what it does, in terms of the functional role it plays. Then empirical research fills in just what it is playing that role. For example, the gene can be defined as the unit of hereditary transmission. Science then discovers that bits of DNA play that role. And so we reduce genes to bits of DNA. This has been a very successful explanatory pattern in the sciences, leading to the current widespread support for physicalism. Many seemingly irreducible phenomena have fallen to reductive explanation in this way. But to deny at the outset that p-consciousness is functional is to cut off this road to reduction and physicalism. Block, however, does not think that this is the only way, or even the usual way, that complex things get reduced down to basic physical bits. The other way to do it is with Smart's simplicity maneuver. We find that two things – for example, lightning and an electromagnetic discharge – always occur at the same time. We are not logically compelled to say they are one and the same thing. Rather, it simplifies our ontology if we do so. So we conclude that lightning just *is* electromagnetic discharge. No functionalization needed.

But will it work for consciousness? Block argues that, instead of starting with a functional analysis of a phenomenon, we simply "point" to exemplars of the thing we're interested in reducing. We then use science to investigate the thing we've pointed at. And science is the final arbiter on what there is – it is the most simple, elegant, explanatorily fruitful picture of the world we've developed. The preliminary step of functional analysis just isn't needed. We just jump right into the science and let the metaphysical chips fall where they may. As we now see, this approach to reductive theorizing differs from that of David Chalmers, which I've used so far to introduce the problem of consciousness. Chalmers, following the work of David Lewis and Frank Jackson, argues that functionalization is a necessary step to reduction.[5] And because we can't functionalize consciousness, dualism follows. But if Block is correct, there's a space left open between functionalism and dualism for the physicalist to locate consciousness. On Block's picture, then, we should proceed in the following way.[6] First, "point" to some good examples of conscious experiences. How do we do that? Access some experiences from the first-person point of view. For example, have someone drop a piano on your foot.[7] The resulting pain is a fine example of a conscious state, one that is hard to miss! Now, while you're doing that, have your brain scanned. If we find that the same region of brain or group of cells or what have you always activate when you're in piano-induced pain, for reasons of simplicity we can conclude that the pain *just is* that neural activity. This is metaphysically simpler than saying there are two things here, the pain and the neural activity. Thus, the dualist view is less simple and the physicalist position is to be favored. And to argue that there's a hidden underlying intrinsic nature at play here is again to add an additional element. So, nonreductive views are less simple, especially if they entail panpsychism with its radical distribution of consciousness. Further, we aren't forced to cram consciousness into an ill-fitting functionalist box.[8]

But how does this approach handle the ever-present threat of zombies? Surely, we can conceive of beings with brains like ours, right down to the neurons, who nonetheless lack consciousness. And doesn't this suggest their real possibility as well? Block has several lines of response to the zombie threat (Block and Stalnaker 1999). First and foremost, as I've just explained, he rejects the model of reductive explanation implicit in the zombie argument. The zombie argument holds that we can tell by a priori analysis of the *concept* of consciousness that the concept rules out mind–brain identity. But Block counters that the whole idea of a priori conceptual analysis is offtrack. Following philosophers like Quine (1951), Block argues that there's no way to isolate the "pure" concept of anything: all our concepts are wrapped up with our worldly empirical knowledge. The best we can do is figure out, in a preliminary and tentative way, what our terms point to in the world. Then we use our best empirical method – science – to figure out what's really out there. It may be that what we thought we were picking out at the beginning of our investigation isn't even present at the end of our studies. We just cannot tell prior to actually doing the science how things are going to *conceptually* turn out. And this is made clear in Block's method of "pointing" at exemplars of access and phenomenal consciousness. He tries his best to offer real-world (or close to real-world) examples to do the pointing. Then we should go off and do the hard work of science. The fact that we can conceive of zombies now tells us little about how the scientific investigation will turn out. And that is our best guide to the possibilities that matter for theorizing about consciousness.

But what of the claim, endorsed by Chalmers, Jackson, and others, that most reductive theorizing works by providing a functional analysis of the phenomenon in question? When we discovered water was just H_2O, for example, didn't this involve a functional analysis of good, old-fashioned water? But Block argues that even this analysis is infected with worldly knowledge. We just can't tell what our words pick out without knowing about the actual world we live in. And that knowledge is a matter of empirical investigation rather than a priori analysis. Here, Block is influenced by the prior work of Hillary Putnam, who argued that the meanings of our words are fundamentally entangled with the things that caused them to be said in the first place.[9] Putnam offers the example of "water" as a case in point (Putnam 1975). If asked to give a conceptual analysis of "water," we might follow Chalmers and others in saying that it's the stuff filling our lakes and rivers, that flows from our taps, that freezes in cold weather and boils when sufficiently heated, and so on. It is the stuff "playing the watery role." And we know this simply by being competent users of the English term "water." But in addition, we *now* know that water is H_2O. How does this matter? Consider an astronaut traveling to another world. She finds a colorless, odorless, drinkable liquid filling the lakes and rivers there. The liquid flows from the taps, freezes in winter, boils when sufficiently heated, and so on. But, unlike the stuff on earth, this liquid's chemical makeup is *not* H_2O; rather, it is XYZ, let's say. Question: is this stuff water? Putnam, Kripke, Block, and many others answer *No*! Water, we now know, is identical to H_2O. And this stuff isn't H_2O, so it isn't water! Full stop. But the facts about H_2O

don't appear in our conceptual analysis. Indeed, if we were following that analysis, we'd have to say that this XYZ stuff *is* water. And that's the wrong answer, according to Block and friends. So the idea that we can tell what's what just by analyzing our concepts "in the armchair" is a mistake.

And how does this impact the zombie argument? Well, the zombie argument holds that we can tell by analysis that zombies are conceivable. Block and Co. agree with that – nothing in our a priori analysis rules them out. But the jump to the real possibility of zombies stalking the landscape doesn't go through. That jump requires the analysis of consciousness alone to really show us how things are. But we don't know how things are, on the Putnam/Block picture, without doing some empirical investigation. For all we can tell from our armchair, a priori, zombies might be possible. But science may show us that consciousness is identical to a brain state, and so, despite what we can conceive, anything with that sort of brain state is conscious. Zombies, in that case, aren't possible, despite being conceivable. Science trumps our everyday conception of consciousness, at least in principle. When we have a good theory of the brain, we'll learn what consciousness really is. And that may rule out the possibility of zombies, however conceivable they may be.

But Block is leaning heavily on the simplifying power of the identity claim. Is that enough to *explain* how brain states account for conscious experience in all its richness? This problem seems especially pressing for Block, as he has adamantly defended a nonfunctional notion of p-consciousness. Where's the explanatory "oomph" in telling us that consciousness *just is* nothing but the firing of pyramidal cells or what have you? In reply, Block argues that we shouldn't be looking for that kind of explanation. Block's identity theory is only *weakly reductive*, in the sense laid out in chapter 1. Block asks us to consider a famous identity claim like Mark Twain = Sam Clemens. Once we have established the identity (for reasons of simplicity, say), there's just no further question of *how* Mark Twain could be Sam Clemens. He just *is* – it's just one guy with two names. There's nothing more to say. A thing just is what it is and not another thing, to paraphrase the old philosophical saw. Looking for more is like asking how Superman could be Clark Kent. Once we get beyond the clever disguise of wearing glasses and a suit, that's it. He just is. Explanation has to end somewhere!

This may not close the explanatory gap completely, but it suggests we're demanding more than we can get if we want a really illuminating explanation of consciousness in physical terms. But, Block argues, we don't often find those in science anyway. Pointing back to Smart once more, Block contends that reduction in science generally is driven by inductive pressures to simplify rather than by deductive, conceptual argument. Lightning and electromagnetic discharges keep occurring together. We can dig in our heels and say there's two things present, or we can help ourselves to the simplifying assumption that there's just one thing here. We may not get a deeper story out of our reductive maneuver, but that's the way things go.

We are left with the claim that consciousness, right down to the qualitative features of p-consciousness, is just brain activity. That best respects our first-person access to experience because it does not illicitly define consciousness as a functional access process. And it respects the sweeping power and success of our scientific worldview without the need for radical revision. There's no need to add to our ontology or to posit things beyond the reach of physical theory. We just have brain states that are identical to conscious states. And we can see the clear role that brain science plays in telling us what consciousness really is. Was it really all that plausible that we could tell just by "peering inward" that consciousness wasn't ultimately something brainy?

But, despite its ontological simplicity, there are serious worries about the identity theory (it's always something!). The view can be attacked from both "sides" – from the more strongly reductive functionalist position and from the anti-reductive perspective as well. The first criticism we'll consider comes from the functionalist side. This will allows us to see one of the main motivations for functionalism (taken up in the next chapter) and to look at a response by what has come to be known as the "new generation" of identity theorists. After that, we'll get back to anti-reduction and the zombie threat, as well as a related problem acknowledged and articulated by Ned Block himself.

Worries, Replies, and More Worries About Identity Theory

An identity claim says that what we thought might be two different things are really just one thing. When we say that Twain = Clemens or Clark = Superman, we're saying that these two guys are really one guy in different outfits. So let's look at the claim being made by the identity theorist. The identity theorist holds that conscious states are identical to brain states. Consider the conscious experience of pain. Let's say we find that whenever a person is in pain, a certain type of neural cell, call them "c-fibers," fires. Following Smart's simplicity suggestion, we get the claim that pain = c-fiber firing. Sweet. But this claim tells us what pain is and what it isn't. If you don't have c-fiber firings, you're not in pain. Because that's just what pain is. And this raises what is called the "multiple realization" worry. Intuitively, we're not the only sorts of creatures who can be in pain. Dogs, cats, wombats, and whales can plausibly be in pain, and it may be that octopuses, cuttlefish, and squids can as well. And perhaps even simpler creatures can. But it may be that these creatures *don't have c-fibers*. Indeed, the anatomy of the range of creatures that may feel pain seems extremely diverse, even if we limit our speculation to currently existing critters on this planet. But if dogs or whales or octopuses don't have c-fibers, then they do not have pain according to the identity theory. Nothing lacking c-fibers can, because that's what pain is, according to the identity theory. And the situation grows far worse if we consider the possibility of aliens. What if an alien landed and we dropped a piano on its tentacles? Imagine that it screamed and writhed and cursed us as it wriggled about. Surely, we'd think it is in pain. But if such a creature lacks c-fibers then it isn't in pain no matter what else is true of it, if the identity theory is right. This seems weird to many. It appears at least an open possibility that something else might "realize" pain in these other creatures. Thus, it is claimed that pain is *multiply realizable* and so the identity theory cannot be correct. Ned Block himself is famous for laying out the details of this sort of objection (Block 1978). He holds that theories concluding that too few things have pains are "chauvinistic," while those letting in too many things are "liberal." The identity theory seems badly chauvinistic. This is the multiple realization objection to the identity theory.

And it isn't just cephalopods and aliens causing trouble. Human brains are marked by a fair degree of "plasticity," the capacity for one region of brain to take over the function of another in certain circumstances. Brain injury, particularly in the young, is sometimes overcome when neighboring regions take over the function of the damaged areas. And this can even occur in older individuals injured by stroke or other neural afflictions. But if one brain region can take over for another, what happens to our identity claims? Imagine that the region where c-fibers reside is damaged and the neighboring region, made up of d-fibers, takes over the function of the injured locale. If this can happen, would it follow that the person wasn't in pain, even if everything the c-fibers did was now taken over by d-fibers? Or can we tell from the original identity claim that such a thing *couldn't possibly happen*? Given our current knowledge of plasticity, it seems wrong to rule out this possibility. But then we get multiple realization within a single human subject. Pain just doesn't seem to be identifiable in the simple way the Smart/Block approach suggests.

But perhaps things aren't so grim for the identity theory. First, it might be argued that the identity claim being offered is much more limited than it first appears. Instead of saying that *all* pain is identical with c-fiber firing, it might just be claiming that *human* pain is identical with c-fiber firings. Octopus or alien pain can then be identified with whatever realizes their pains. This move is a bit worrisome when we consider the possibility of different realizations among different human populations (Texan pains? French pains?). This may cut things too finely. And it's worse when we take up the plasticity worry (Josh's pains now vs. Josh's post-accident pains?). But maybe the threat of multiple realization is overblown. Too many philosophers, some argue, have read too much into the multiple realization problem and use it as an excuse to ignore the brain altogether. If pain is multiply realizable, then it's not identical to any brain state and we should consider it on a more abstract functional picture (pain states are states that do the right sort of thing, whatever they're realized in). A new wave of identity theorists criticizes this move and calls for us to get back to the brain!

Following the lead of philosopher Patricia Churchland and her 1986 book *Neurophilosophy*, new-wave identity theorists argue that when we look closely at neuroscience, we find that the neural identity theory is widely embraced as a means of explaining the mind and that worries of multiple realization do not impede progress in the field.[10] Many of the studies illuminating how our brains work actually use nonhuman subjects. Monkeys are the main victims, but other critters are used as well. And we find that the same *neural structures* are present in these other creatures, allowing us to successfully extrapolate from the nonhuman cases to our own. So, in general, scientific practice relies on neural identity, rather than multiply realized function, to do its business. To return to the toy example, we posit an identity between c-fiber firings and pain, study c-fiber firings in rats, and then successfully extrapolate to humans. It's the common presence of the neural realizer that provides the explanatory kick. This lessens the threat of multiple realization, unless we are worried about science fiction aliens.

What's more, when we do find differences in the underlying neural substrate, we generally find differences in the functional behavior of systems as well. Take the case of vision, for example. An identity claim might have it that conscious vision is identical to a certain type of neural architecture involving a specific type of cell. But, the multiple realization worry goes, what about vision in very different creatures, like our friends the octopuses and the bees? However, when we look at how vision functions in those creatures, we find that it isn't the same as how it works in us or other mammals. So we get what the identity theory predicted: different stuff, different mental process. There isn't, it appears, just one type of thing that is *vision*, a thing that can be multiply realized. Rather, there are lots of subtypes of vision and they are identical to the various realizers in their respective critters. Now what makes them all types of vision is an interesting question and here a functionalist answer may be appropriate. But if we want to be metaphysically (and explanatorily) precise, human vision is identical to certain neural states in us, octopus vision is identical to certain different neural processes in them, and so on.

Interestingly, this type of new-wave neural identity theory is often strongly reductive. Patricia Churchland and John Bickle, for example, defend strong neural reductionist views in the mind, including consciousness. We met Churchland in chapter 2 when we discussed her optimistic mysterianism. There, she held that once we get all the facts about the brain, we'll have the whole story, without remainder. Bickle is certainly on board in spirit. But Block, famously, defends the specialness of p-consciousness and rejects any strongly reductive program. In the end, he doesn't think Churchland's or Bickle's neural optimism will play out. Rather, we'll be left with a brute, simplifying reduction, one that doesn't explain but just cleans up our ontology. It seems that Churchland and Bickle (among others in the new neural identity camp) are open to a kind of "neural functionalization" of p-consciousness: when we understand how the human brain functions, we'll understand p-consciousness. But Block's view does not license even this neural functionalization.

However, Block's rejection of functionalization leaves him open to attack from the zombies. If all we have is the thin reed of simplification, why not think that the temporal coincidence of pain and c-fibers is just that, a coincidence, rather than an indication of identity? Without a reductive explanatory link telling us *why* c-fibers realize conscious pains, the identity claim seems just to be an article of faith on the part of the weakly reductive identity theorist. Further, Chalmers argues that without this reductive link, the tight connection of metaphysical identity – the sort of identity we're after here, identity that really pins down what a thing is in a fundamental sense – is merely a "brute" connection.[11] That is not meant as a compliment. A brute identity is one that doesn't follow from the logic of the terms, even if we know all about what our terms mean *and* all about what there is in the real world. Chalmers contends that, in all other cases of macro-level phenomena where we have both these sorts of information, the explanatory gap between the two things identified closes. If we know that "water" means the stuff playing the watery role here and we know that the stuff playing that role is H_2O, then we know that water is H_2O. Likewise, if we know the stuff playing that role is XYZ, then we know that water is XYZ (assuming that's what it has always been here, contrary to fact). But on the weakly reductive identity, we know what the term "pain" picks out and we know, for example, that c-fiber firings are always present when we feel pain. Still, the open question of *why* c-fiber firings feel painful persists. And that, Chalmers contends, is unique in our knowledge. But this suggests that all one can say in favor of the identity is that it's an article of physicalist faith. At this point, Chalmers argues, we're better off accepting the gap as real and going nonreductive.

Block, as I noted above, rejects Chalmers overall setup of meaning and knowledge – we shouldn't expect there to be the a priori entailment and reduction Chalmers demands. But there is something that still does not sit well if all we have is a nonexplanatory identity claim. Indeed, this shortcoming is an inspiration for strongly reductive views to follow. And it's not that we want to know how it could be that Clark Kent is Superman, given that there's just one guy here. We want to know, rather, how this guy, wearing glasses or not, can *fly*! And that's left wanting on Block's view. So perhaps Chalmers is going too far in suggesting that we can tell from the armchair whether or not a "complete" theory closes the explanatory gap, but we can still see that there's an explanatory itch that's left itching on Block's weakly reductive view.

But Block has another card to play here. Block (and other identity theorists) notes that the explanatory gap is driven by the disparity between our two ways of thinking about consciousness: accessing it from the outside, from a third-person perspective, and accessing from the inside, from a first-person perspective. This difference in access helps explain why we retain an explanatory itch even when presented with a simplifying identity claim. On this view, first-person access is mediated by special "phenomenal concepts," concepts in part *constituted by* conscious experience.[12] So, when I see red, for example, I have a red phenomenal state and I reflect on it by embedding that very state in a phenomenal concept. One way to think of phenomenal concepts is that they "bracket" phenomenal states themselves, without redescribing or representing them in any other terms. They "point" like demonstrative terms: "I am in *that* state," where the "that" slot is filled by phenomenal redness itself, by a red "quale." So we directly access the redness in first-person awareness, but when we think of the same quality theoretically, from the third-person perspective, no such embedding occurs. Thus, it may seem that we just can't be talking about the same thing here!

While this so-called "phenomenal concepts strategy" does say more about why we find the identity claim mysterious, it does not close off the problem altogether. We can still ask, *why* is it that when we "embed" a phenomenal state in a cognitive "bracket" that it reveals itself to us in the distinctive way we experience? And, again, how could any neural state do this sort of thing in the first place? Either we've still got an undischarged and unexplained phenomenal element lurking, or we need to provide a functional explanation of phenomenal concepts, including the phenomenal element. But we can't do that without remainder, given Block's anti-functionalization claim for p-consciousness. So, it seems, we're left in pretty much the same explanatory bind as we were before.

And this worry is brought out in a slightly different way by Block himself. Block argues that there is a "harder" problem of consciousness (Block 2002). He contends that the hard problem – the challenge of saying why some neural process is conscious rather than not – is solved by the identity theory. But still, we are left with a very strange epistemological puzzle, if we are committed to several things Block holds dear. One is the claim that p-consciousness can't be functionalized. Two is the truth of the identity claim. And three is a commitment to *naturalism*, the idea that we must stick to the methods of natural science in figuring out what there is. Commitment to these three claims makes the problem of *alien* consciousness extremely problematic. This is the harder problem. Block focuses on an android, Data from *Star Trek: The Next Generation*. Data is clearly intelligent and in some episodes even has emotions (he has a special "emotion chip" installed). But we might wonder whether he is conscious or not. How, given commitment to Block's three theses, could we figure this out? Since functionalism is out, we can't simply look at how his "positronic brain" functions. And since we're identity theorists, we can't appeal to what Data is made of – he's not made of the same stuff as us, so that's out. But this seems like a legitimate open question. Maybe he's conscious, even if it's not quite the same as our human consciousness.

But there just seems to be no way at all for the naturalist to proceed here! Science, it appears, just can't answer this question. There is a blind spot in the naturalist's vision of the world. Functionalists reject number one (and, generally, number two) of Block's theses and develop functionalist theories with at least the chance of answering the question based on how Data functions. Anti-reductionists give up number three, generally, though "naturalistic dualists" like Chalmers try to hold onto three while giving up on number two. (Recall that the naturalistic dualist must have linking principles connecting function to consciousness in *our* world, though not in other distant metaphysically possible worlds.) Block wants to keep all three so he's left with a puzzle, the harder problem, as puts it. Maybe this is just something the naturalist can't know. Or maybe in the future we'll figure something out, to play the moderate mysterian card. But something seems to be missing from Block's picture.

The Distinction Between A-Consciousness and P-Consciousness, One Last Time

One final point needs to be addressed in this chapter, as a lead in to the functionalist position. Block's whole view is predicated on the real distinction between a-consciousness and p-consciousness and on the nonfunctional nature of p-consciousness. In his initial presentation of the distinction, Block used thought experiments and anecdotal evidence to support the distinction. Functionalists had ready responses to those attempts. More recently, Block has pushed an empirical defense of the distinction, based on a series of results in cognitive science (Block 2008; 2011a). The most discussed case is taken from the work of Sperling (1960). Sperling had subjects look at an array of letters laid out in a four-column by three-row grid. The first task was to report as many of the letters as one could remember after a short presentation. The average result was three or four. Next, Sperling added a tone, high, middle, or low, just after the grid disappeared. Now the subject's job was to report just the letters in the row indicated by the tone. For instance, if they hear the high tone, they report the top row. Subjects could do this with much greater accuracy – they could get a whole row right, even though they didn't know beforehand which row would be cued. This suggests that subjects have a "buffer" memory of the stimulus that they can still access even after it has disappeared, with all twelve letters present.

So how does this show p-consciousness is separate from a-consciousness? Block contends that we are p-conscious of all the letters in the grid – there is something it's like for us to see them all. But we can only access a limited set of them, around four. So p-consciousness "overflows" access, showing that the two are distinct. Block bases this on two factors. The first is performance. We must see all the letters so that we can do equally well no matter which row is cued by the tone. And this is confirmed in the study. High, middle, or low, it doesn't matter. We can name the four in that row. But we don't know beforehand which row will be cued while the letters are visible. So we must see them all in memory. But once we access a row, we have exhausted the flow of access, removing our ability to report on the other rows. And that is confirmed as well. The best we can do is four letters or so. So phenomenality outruns access and the two are distinct. What's more, Block notes that he's been a subject in the experiment and he can report that it sure seems to him that he sees all the letters! But, like other subjects, he could only access a subset for reporting. So phenomenology, as well as behavior, confirms the overflow.

But, perhaps unsurprisingly at this point, Block's opponents from the functionalist side have a response (see, for example, Cohen and Dennett 2011). They contend that the memory store of the letters is *unconscious*, and we then access from that unconscious store what we need when cued. Our p-conscious experience may *seem* to have been of all the specific letters, but it wasn't. Rather, we knew that there were letter-shaped forms there, but not exactly what letters they were. The processing of the specific identities of the letters goes on out of conscious awareness, despite how it seems to Block. So memory might outrun p-consciousness, but p-consciousness does not outrun access. Note that this requires an explanation of why things seemed clearer to subjects than they were. But that story may be a necessary bit of functionalism, as we'll see in the next chapter.

For now, we can conclude that the task of establishing the a-consciousness/p-consciousness distinction is still up in the air. But given that many accept it, Block's identity theory may be the best way to go to defend a physicalist theory of consciousness, even if such an approach is lacking in explanatory kick. But for those holding out for whole explanatory enchilada, the final three chapters are for you. We'll look at three versions of strong reductionism in turn: functionalism, first-order representationalism, and higher-order representationalism. Zombies beware! We may solve the hard problem yet!

Further Reading

J. J. C. Smart's 1959 paper "Sensations and Brain Processes" is an excellent starting point for this literature. Block's 1995 "On a Confusion about a Function of Consciousness," as well as his 2002 "Harder Problem of Consciousness," are both important pieces and do a good job of presenting Block's important view. Patricia Churchland's *Neurophilosophy* and John Bickle's *Psychoneural Reduction: The New Wave*, as well as his *Stanford Encyclopedia of Philosophy* entry on multiple realizability, are all excellent sources for the new wave of identity theorists and the prospects of a stronger reductive identity claim than that of Block.

6
Functionalism

Functionalism is the view that the mind is defined by what it does, not by what it's made of. If you "do the right thing", you're in. The identity theory, by contrast, says you need "the right stuff" (to stick with the 1980s' movie titles). The possibility of multiple realization is one of the main motivations for functionalism. It seems plausible to think that lots of different kinds of creatures can have experiences, even if they're made of very different kinds of stuff. And for those who are open to the possibility of machine minds or even machine consciousness, functionalism seems to be a requirement. Functionalism as I've characterized it so far is a very broad view, taking in a range of positions. In fact, the views we'll consider in the following two chapters – first-order representationalism and higher-order representationalism – are versions of functionalism in this broad sense. But because they highlight the function of representing, either the world or the subject's own states, those views get separate treatment. In this chapter, we'll focus on "purer" examples of functionalism, ones framed in terms of what consciousness *does* for its subjects. We'll first look at a number of ways of pinpointing the right functional "level" to describe the mind. Then we'll consider some examples of functionalist theories of consciousness, most notably the "global workspace" view. But we'll also look at what are known as "enactive" or "extended" views of consciousness. These are versions of functionalism taking the relevant functional roles to extend beyond the head to the rest of the body and even the outside environment. We'll close, as usual, with some worries about the view, most notably that functionalists aren't even talking about consciousness! They are, according to some critics (and even some proponents), "eliminativists" about consciousness. With that in mind, before even looking at the question of the right functional "level" to focus on, we need to address just what consciousness is supposed to be on a functionalist theory.

A Functional Characterization of Consciousness

So far, the views we've considered have all held that consciousness is something special because, among other things, it cannot be given a functional analysis. Indeed, this is the heart of the zombie worry. If consciousness could be given an adequate functional definition, then we would be able to rule out zombies altogether from the start because they function just as we do. Functionalists think we can give just such a characterization, one that fully captures in functional terms what we mean by "consciousness," without remainder. But isn't it just obvious that they're wrong? Wouldn't that show not just that zombies aren't possible, but that they aren't even *conceivable*, a much stronger claim?

Functionalists can handle this worry in one of two ways. The first is to take it head on and say, yes, we're actually claiming that, despite what others may claim, zombies are in fact inconceivable. Are you so sure that if you really focus on a being that does *everything* we do, right down to holding all the same beliefs, desires, goals, and dreams, that it wouldn't just be a conscious being? How could a being do all that we do without being conscious? What seems prima facie conceivable may turn out not to be on more careful reflection. It might take a fair bit of careful, reflective thought to discover that the idea of zombies conflicts with other things we hold to be true. Or perhaps the very idea of a zombie is internally incoherent in a way we've yet to uncover. If so, then again, zombies are only prima facie conceivable, but not really conceivable.

The other tactic for functionalists is to accept that we can conceive of zombies, but hold that this is because our naive view of consciousness is confused. Once we straighten it out, we'll see that a functionalist analysis is the way to go and, therefore, zombies are inconceivable. In other words, we may have confused ideas about our own minds, and on this basis come to think consciousness possesses special nonfunctional features. Then we imagine beings lacking these nonfunctional features, features we never possessed to begin with! It might even be that a functionalist theory out-and-out *predicts* that we'd be confused in this way, given the way our mental architecture is set up. On this approach, we can conceive of zombies, but that tells us nothing about how things must be, because we're operating under a kind of illusion, the illusion that consciousness has special nonfunctional elements. Once we get things straight, we'll see that zombies are irrelevant. It may be that we'll never shake the feeling that something is missing from a functionalist account. But that's OK, so long as we know that this feeling isn't to be taken seriously. Or maybe our distant offspring, raised in the glorious functionalist future, will find it obvious that zombies are inconceivable. However, we old fogies will never get it, sadly. There is much more to say about this matter and we'll take it up again when we consider the eliminativist worry at the end of the chapter. For now, we'll allow that a functionalist program can at least get off the ground without being eaten by zombies.

What Functional Roles Matter for Consciousness?

The idea of a functionalist theory of consciousness, then, is that if a mental state plays the right functional role, it is a conscious state. But how are we to determine what the right "role" is for consciousness? There are lots of ways to think about the functional roles of mental states. Most basically, we can think of them as being defined by causal connections to the right sorts of inputs and outputs, as well as the right sorts of connections to other mental states. We might characterize the inputs, outputs, and connections in *commonsense* terms, in the terms of our everyday "folk psychology."[1] For example, a pain might be the sort of state that is caused by having pianos dropped on your foot, by paper cuts, bee stings, stubbed toes, etc.; that causes screaming, writhing, hopping up and down, vigorous rubbing, etc.; and that cause the desire for the feeling to stop, the belief that this sucks, interferes with the ability to do math, etc. If a state does all this – and note that it might take a gigantic amount of space to fill in the ellipses here – then it is a pain state. And likewise for states like belief and desire, for wishes, hopes, fears, and so on. We use the input, output, and interaction profile to specify the mental state in terms of its functional role. Because this method appeals to the ordinary, everyday inputs, outputs, and interactions, it's known as "commonsense functionalism."

But that's not the only way to fill out the three clauses. Instead of looking to common sense, we might appeal to science to tell us what count as the right inputs, outputs, and interactions.[2] For example, a pain might be a state caused by activation of damage detection systems, causing aversive reactions and interfering with other cognitive processes. Or pains might be caused by activation of a specific type of neuron connected to damage detection systems, causing the firing of neurons in the motor cortex implicated in avoidance routines, and causing a flood of hormonal reactions, inhibiting the functioning of non-essential processing. And so on. We can look to cognitive psychology, physiology, or neuroscience to provide the three clauses. So long as we are still thinking in terms of what the system does, rather than what it's made of, we're in a functionalist frame of mind. But note that as we get more and more involved with brain function, rather than more broadly construed functional roles, we run the risk of being "chauvinistic," of ruling out creatures without our sort of nervous system from feeling pain. But we can then retreat to a theory of human pain, rather than pain in general. The differences between fine-grained neural-functionalism and a functionally motivated identity theory are minimal, upon close examination.

But there is a much more abstract way to characterize function, and it's one that sits at the heart of much of

cognitive science: a computational approach.[3] We can con-
strue the inputs, outputs, and interactions in terms of computations. If a system takes certain values as inputs, goes
through a number of interactive functions, and then produces
certain values as outputs, we might say that it is adding. Or
calculating the route to the nearest pub. Or, to return to our
example, feeling pain. This, in somewhat caricatured form,
is the way artificial intelligence might functionally characterize the mind. Computers are prime examples of functionally
characterizable systems. A computer program takes certain
input, goes through various transformations, and delivers
certain outputs. It may be that logical, rational thinking can
be unpacked in this way. And this has led some to think that
all mental states ought to be specifiable in this manner, even
states like pains. At this level of abstraction, we can feel
strongly the lurking danger of zombies. Even if a machine
made all the right moves, even if it produced ever so realistic
"screams" after we drop a piano on its foot, it seems at best
an open question whether it's feeling pain at all. Simply going
through the right series of computations does not seem adequate to produce the "ouchiness" of pain. This is the main
worry about functionalism, and this abstract, computer-
inspired version is known as "machine functionalism."[4]

And finally, there is a more radical approach to fixing the
roles that matter for a theory of consciousness. So far, all the
views we've considered take mental states to be things inside
the head, ultimately to be realized by brain processes. But an
alternative picture holds that mental states themselves are not
just in the head, but extend outward into our bodies and the
wider world. It's not just that what we think is causally connected to our bodies and environments. It's that our thinking
is in part *made* of our bodies and environments. Minds,
including conscious minds, just ain't in the head, on this
view.[5] But what kinds of roles are the right ones? Take an
example of consciously walking through a forest. We experience the flow of the trees as they sweep past, we move
through the dappled sunlight and deeper shade, we avoid
obstacles and slow to focus on interesting minutia. On the
standard view, we are constantly building inner models and
representations of the world around us and updating them as
new info streams in. But on the "extended" alternative, there

is no need to actively recreate the outer world inside us. Instead, we are constantly and synergistically engaged in a kind of reciprocal dance with the outside world. We are wrapped up with it in a series of feedback loops and dependencies. The world itself serves as what we see, not some inner model. And because we have developed deep anticipatory connections between what we see now and what we would see if we moved in this or that way, the world is seen in all its richness, even if we don't "bring it inside." On this sort of view, if a creature is properly embedded in its environment, in such a way that it can exploit the stable "affordances" of the things around it, then it is in a conscious state. This still counts as a version of functionalism on the way I've put things because if you do the right thing – if you dance with your environment in the right way – you're a conscious state, even if that state is in part made of the environment you're conscious of. It takes two to tango!

What is the Function of Consciousness?

But is it possible, then, to find the unique functional role of consciousness? The zombie worry looms. But psychologist Bernard Baars, one of the main developers of the most worked-out and well-defined functionalist view, the "global workspace theory," provides a useful method for isolating the right functional role (Baars 1988). He calls it the "contrastive method." We look for a matched pair of mental states, with one member conscious and the other not. Then, we can consider what difference being conscious makes to the mental state. This difference provide the functional role of consciousness in us. And we find, according to Baars, that conscious states are available to a wide range of mental capacities while unconscious states are restricted to more limited local processing. If I consciously see a cell phone, I can reason about it in all sorts of ways, plan and execute a variety of cell-phone-directed behaviors, reflect on how the cell phone looks like mine, and so on. But if I only subliminally detect the cell phone, I might prepare my hand in the right configuration to grab it and I might prime various cell-phone related thoughts.

But I won't have the broad, open-ended mental flexibility I have when I see it consciously. Baars takes this to mean that the functional role of consciousness is to globally "broadcast" information, enabling a battery of flexible responses. If you play this role, you are a conscious state. Consciousness, on this picture, is global access and a conscious state is one that is globally accessible. We'll look at the details of this view in a moment, including a neural version of the view defended by neuroscientist Stanislas Dehaene and colleagues. But, for now, we'll consider other ideas about the functional role of consciousness.

Daniel Dennett holds that conscious states are states winning the competition for brain-wide resources (Dennett 1991; 2005). When a state achieves this "fame in the brain," it becomes conscious. Fame is a nice metaphor here because it is a relational, rather than an intrinsic, property. You are famous because of how you're connected to everyone else. Fame isn't something you can have alone in your room, alas. When a mental state achieves this sort of "fame," it gets "talked about" by other systems; it gets remembered, at least for the short term but maybe for the long haul; it is most likely to get "publicity" in active behavior, including verbal behavior; and it gains certain perks, like determining what the person does next. If you do all this, you achieve fame in the brain – you are a conscious state.

A more basic, computer-inspired way to think of the functional role of consciousness is to see it as a kind of availability to an "executive system" (Schacter 1989). An executive system is the part of the mind setting long-term goals, making decisions in difficult cases, and deciding what will be stored, ignored, or acted upon. Conscious states, on this view, are states inputted to the executive system. Or perhaps they are states *available* for executive action. They may be held in a special "working memory," a short-term store where thoughts and perceptions are held pending action by the executive system. It may be that merely being available in this way to the executive system is enough to make a state conscious. In addition, there does seem to be a tight connection between a state's being *reportable* and its being conscious (Dennett 1978). If we can verbally report that we're in a state, that state is conscious. So it may be that accessibility to the reporting system is key to consciousness. This might seem to limit consciousness to those who can make verbal reports, but we can reasonably expand the range of the proposal by looking for related or more primitive versions of that sort of functional architecture.

Finally, an external "extended" functionalism defines conscious states in terms of the right complex of mind–body–world interactions. If a creature is appropriately embedded in its environment and is able to extract a range of usable information relevant to its goals, then it is in a conscious state (Noë 2005). Focusing again on the difference between conscious and unconscious states, we find that conscious states are far richer in their reciprocal, interactive connections to the environment. We may be able to do a lot unconsciously, but we won't be able to take advantage of all the meaningful goal-related information in our environment. Nor can we deal effectively with novel stimuli, with things popping up where we least expect them. Consciousness allows us to bring to bear a range of complex skills we couldn't access while on "autopilot." This rich sort of interactive engagement *constitutes* our conscious state on the "extended" functionalist view. With these functional roles in hand, we'll now take a closer look at some of the prominent functionalist theories of consciousness. Then we'll close by focusing on some of the worries plaguing the functionalist view.

Functionalist Theories of Consciousness

Perhaps the best developed empirical theory of consciousness is the global workspace view (Baars 1988; 1997). The basic idea is that conscious states are defined by their "promiscuous accessibility," by being available to the mind in ways that nonconscious states are not. If a state is nonconscious, you just can't do that much with it. It will operate automatically along relatively fixed lines. However, if the state is conscious, it connects with the rest of our mental lives, allowing for the generation of far more complex behavior. The global workspace (GWS) idea takes this initial insight and develops a psychological theory – one pitched at the level of cognitive science, involving a high-level decomposition of the mind into functional units. The view has also been connected to a range of data in neuroscience, bolstering its plausibility. The multileveled success of an empirical theory like GWS may be the best way to counter the worry that something nonfunctional is left out of a theory of consciousness. Zombie beware!

So, how does the theory go? First, the GWS view stresses the idea that much of our mental processing occurs *modularly*. Modules are relatively isolated, "encapsulated" mechanisms devoted to solving limited, "domain-specific" problems.[6] Modules work largely independently from each other and they are not open to "cross talk" coming from outside their focus of operation. A prime example is how the early vision system works to create the 3-D array we consciously experience. Our early-vision modules automatically take cues from the environment and deliver rapid output concerning what's in front of us. For example, some modules detect edges, some the intersection of lines or "vertices," some subtle differences in binocular vision, and so on. To work most efficiently, these modules employ built-in assumptions about what we're likely to see. In this way, they can quickly take an ambiguous cue and deliver a reliable output about what we're seeing. But this increase in speed leads to the possibility of error when the situation is not as the visual system assumes. In the Müller-Lyer illusion, two lines of the same length look unequal because of either inward- or outward-facing "points" on the end of the lines. And even if we know they're the same length, because we've seen these dang lines hundreds of times, we still consciously see them as unequal.[7] This is because the process of detecting the lines takes the vertices where the points attach to the lines as cues about depth. In the real world, when we see such vertices, we can reliably use them to tell us what's closer to what. But the Müller-Lyer illusion uses this fact to trick early vision into seeing things incorrectly. The process is modular because it works automatically and it's immune to correction from our conscious beliefs about the lines.

Modularity is held to be a widespread phenomenon in the mind.[8] Just how widespread is a matter of considerable debate, but most researchers would accept that at least some processes are modular, and early perceptual processes are the best candidates. The idea of the GWS is that the workspace allows us to connect and integrate knowledge from a number of modular systems. This gives us much more flexible control of what we do. And this cross-modular integration would be especially useful to a mind more and more overloaded with modular processes. Hence, we get an evolutionary rationale for the development of a GWS: when modular processing becomes too unwieldy and when the complexity of the tasks we must perform increases, there will be advantages to having a cross-modular GWS.

Items in the global workspace are like things posted on a message board or a public blog. All interested parties can access the information there and act accordingly. They can also alter the info by adding their own input to the workspace. The GWS is also closely connected to short-term working memory. Things held in the workspace can activate working memory, allowing us to keep conscious percepts in mind as we work on problems. Also, the GWS is deeply intertwined with attention. We can activate attention to focus on specific items in the network. But attention can also influence what gets into the workspace in the first place. Things in the network can exert a global "top-down" influence on the rest of the mind, allowing for coordination and control that couldn't be achieved by modules in isolation. To return to a functionalist way of putting things, if a system does what the GWS does, then the items in that system are conscious. That's what consciousness amounts to.

And there is a wide range of neural support for the GWS hypothesis (Dehaene and Naccache 2001). In the brain, we find groups of "network neurons" projecting to many regions of the brain. These neurons take their input largely from sensory cortices and project to the frontal regions of the brain. These higher cortical regions, in turn, take the information and make it available to many other brain areas. What's more, there seems to be a good correlation between absence of activity in these regions and absence of consciousness. Subjects in coma or in a dreamless sleep apparently lack activation of this neural network, supporting the idea that these interconnected areas make up the GWS and that GWS activation is correlated with experience.

Taken together, we get a robust, coherent picture. Much mental activity is nonconscious, occurring in low-level modules. However, when modular information is "taken up" by the GWS, it becomes available to a wide range of mental systems, allowing for flexible top-down control. This is the functional mark of consciousness. And brain data arguably provide support for the picture. Indeed, David Chalmers, one of the main *opponents* to a functional reduction of consciousness concedes that it seems likely that consciousness is *correlated*, in us, with global accessibility. He contends that we can study consciousness empirically if we allow that there are basic laws linking phenomenal consciousness to functional process like global access. If those laws are in place, he thinks that the best candidate at present for the neural correlates of consciousness is something along the lines of the GWS. This of course leaves the question of the strong reduction of consciousness to one side.[9]

The more radical "extended" functionalist alternative takes consciousness out of the head and extends it into the body and the environment. On Alva Noë's version of the view, consciousness is the right sort of rich, interactive "dance" with the world around us. We should not, he urges, try to identify consciousness with some neural state, nor should we reduce it to some inner functional process. Instead, we should consider consciousness (conscious perception, at least) to be a kind of skilled reciprocal embrace of the world around us. He writes "Consciousness is not something that happens in us. It is something we do" (2005: 216). Rather than thinking of consciousness as a spotlight shown on some inner state, we should think about dancing. As Noë puts it,

> A much better image is that of the dancer. A dancer is locked into an environment, responsive to music, responsive to a partner. The idea that the dance is a state of us, inside of us, or something that happens in us is crazy. Our ability to dance depends on all sorts of things going on inside of us, but that we are dancing is fundamentally an attunement to the world around us. (2008)

We wouldn't look into a leg to try and find dancing; likewise, we shouldn't look into the head to try and find consciousness!

Noë's theory focuses on a particular kind of practical skilled-based knowledge, our knowledge of "sensory-motor contingencies," the way that our motor behavior – how we alter the position of our bodies – influences what we perceive. This knowledge is rooted not just in the brain structures involved in perception and action, but in the body and its "muscle memory" of effective engagement with the world around us. On this view, we can employ the environment itself to store information for further use. There is no need to posit snapshots in the brain. In support of this idea, we can note that sufferers of age-related dementia fare far worse memory-wise when they are taken out of their homes and put into unfamiliar care facilities. In their own homes, years of habit have been built up, making it far easier to find things. The home itself stores the information for them. Proponents of this view favor the slogan "The world is its own best model." Taking these strands together, consciousness amounts to the skillful application of embedded, extended sensory-motor knowledge. When we dance like that, we're conscious. We don't actively represent the world. Instead, we have the fast-acting "muscle memory" that the things we're seeing are present in our environments and manipulable in a range of useful ways. There is no need to form "inner pictures" of them – they're available to us in the world when we need them.[10]

Functionalism, in both its more traditional "inner" form and its more radical "outer" version, focuses our attention of activity, on the doing of things. Consciousness is not a static feature of mind, a glowing qualitative gumdrop latched on to brain states. It is the process of accessing ourselves and the world in the right way. What's more, the functionalist view opens the door (for good or ill) to a wider range of conscious critters. If you do the right thing, you're in. Consciousness is as consciousness does, to paraphrase Daniel Dennett. Further, the scientific approach of psychology, physiology, neurology, and much of biology is already functionalist in the broad sense of the term as I'm using it here. To find out how things work in psychology, we figure out what causes what. And we do this by breaking complex things down into the causal interactions of functionally specified parts. A circulatory system is something that spreads nutrients and removes waste in a creature. And a heart is no more than a pump in that system. Do that, and you're a heart. No need for anything more. So a functionalist theory of consciousness, if we can make good on one, lends itself to integration and reduction in the sciences.[11] Indeed, Chalmers recognizing this fact, argues that it's the failure of functionalization that leads most directly to the hard problem. If we can pull off the strongly reductive functionalization of consciousness, the hard problem goes away.

Troubles for Functionalism

But that's just the worry for the many critics of the functionalist approach. According to its critics, the view just changes the subject and provides a theory of this different thing. We wanted to know about *consciousness*, about *what it's like for a subject*. And all we get is workspaces and environmentally embedded dances. Sure, if you define your subject in easy terms to begin with, you can solve any problem. But, as Bertrand Russell stressed, that has "all the advantages of theft over honest toil." Chalmers's way of pushing this point is to argue that functionalists must deny the very *conceivability* of zombies, not just their possibility. But we can already tell, he contends, that zombies are at least conceivable. So functionalism must be wrong. Chalmers's point is that our ability to conceive of zombies shows that our current concept of consciousness just isn't functional. And without a functional concept of consciousness, functionalism can't even get off the ground. So the functionalist must argue for a revised concept of consciousness. But who cares about that, at least in the context of the hard problem? It seems that by changing the subject, functionalism is exposed as a version of eliminativism, the claim that there is no such thing as consciousness after all. If there's no such thing as consciousness, then we might well be able to develop a theory about whatever is left. But this seems an empty victory. As Chalmers puts it, "One might well define 'world peace' as 'a ham sandwich.' Achieving world peace becomes much easier, but it is a hollow achievement" (1996: 105). Of course, the functionalist can retort that we can define "a ham sandwich" as "world peace," making it very hard to get lunch. But this game is being played at the level of "conceptual analysis," of trying to find what our terms really mean. And Chalmers seems to have home field advantage here.[12]

Still, as we noted at the beginning of the chapter, functionalists can argue that the current concept of consciousness is confused or bunk, and so we should switch to something better. Further, they can argue that at least some of our ordinary thinking about consciousness is functional. We *do* think it makes a functional difference that a state is conscious rather than not, at least prima facie. It's not that consciousness makes *no* difference. And this distinction is what definitions like Baars's are trying to capture. So maybe we don't have to junk the whole folk conception of consciousness. It might be a minor touch up, rather than a total teardown. Further, it might be that we'll amend or change our folk concept of consciousness as science progresses. It's not that science has no influence on our everyday thinking, especially when it comes to the mind. Everyone these days speaks about "denial" and "repression," as well as the impact of low blood sugar on moods, lack of serotonin on sleep patterns, and so on – scientific conceptions all. These things move into our ordinary understanding, gradually and pervasively. Perhaps after, say, one thousand years of functionalist brain science, it may become common knowledge that consciousness is accessibility in a global workspace or is the right sort of embedded environmental "dance." And then zombies won't seem even conceivable. So Chalmers's armchair analysis may not stand up in the long term. But it's fair to say that many find the functionalist attempt at a definition of consciousness to be wrong-headed. This pushes folks back towards the weaker reductive position of the identity theory, or even out to the nonreductive approaches. However, as we'll see in the final two chapters, representationalist views may have a better way of framing the functionalist case.

But there are other worries about functionalism as it's been presented here, even if we waive the zombie issue. One main worry concerns the use of *dispositional* terms in the functional definition of consciousness. As we saw in chapter 4, dispositional terms tell us what a thing is likely to do in certain circumstances, even if those circumstances have not actually occurred. A prime example, again, is "fragility." Something is fragile if it is disposed to break when acted upon by a moderate amount of force. Of course, something can be fragile even if it is not broken. It's just that *if* the thing were hit in a certain way, it would likely break. The key dispositional term at play in the functionalist theories we've looked at is "availability." Items in the GWS are conscious when they are available to a range of subsystems. But note that they do not actually have to be accessed by anything. Being available is enough. But, the worry goes, why should the addition of an unactualized disposition make any difference to how things seem to a subject? Isn't consciousness an "occurrent" or categorical property, one that must actually be doing something, not merely be poised to do something? If the information is broadcast but no one is listening, how can it be conscious? Or worse, if it's "broadcastable" but as of yet unbroadcast, how would that serve to "turn on the radio," so to speak?

Functionalists can respond that being in the GWS is an active, categorical property. The network must be active, which means that a bunch of nodes in the network have to fire to hold the information in place. And this is what consciousness amounts to: an active presence in the workspace, no matter what happens next. Normally, there will indeed be "downstream" processing of active network items, but, even if there isn't, there is real, occurrent activity in the GWS itself, which, by the way, can be observed in fMRI scanning. The question may devolve to that of why is it that active presence in the network makes something conscious, but that's more a version of the zombie challenge and not a new worry.

However, there is an overarching worry all functionalists must address. It can be termed the "weird realization" problem and it directly challenges the idea of multiple realization at the core of functionalism. Ned Block famously puts the worry in terms of the nation of China, so this problem is more commonly known as the worry of the "China brain" (Block 1978). Block notes that all that really matters for functionalist views is that the right inputs, outputs, and internal connections are realized. It doesn't matter what realizes them. So, imagine that each citizen of China is given a cell phone and special instructions about how to communicate with other members of the population. We could in (meta-physical!) principle set things up so the pattern of communications exactly parallels the connections of a human brain, functionally characterized. That is, we could have each citizen of China play the functional role of one neuron.[13] Each neuron is connected to a set of others and either fires or does not in specific circumstances. Instead of firing, the citizen of China calls the relevant set of other citizens and they in turn either call others or they don't, depending on their specified role. Now, imagine that we have the entire nation of China emulate the functional activity of the brain of a person eating delicious dim sum. According to Block, so long as the right inputs, outputs, and interactions are properly realized, the functionalist must say that the nation of China, as a whole, is having the same experience as a single person eating dim sum, right down to the savory taste experience of a hot juicy bun! But, Block contends, this is absurd. Why would anyone think this is the case? Functionalism, particularly as a theory of conscious experience, appears much too "liberal" – it lets in too many things as conscious minds.

In response, some functionalists simply accept that *if* you can really get the citizens of China to set up the right functional architecture, then, sure, you have a conscious mind. The incalculable difficulties of doing so explain why we intuitively feel it's impossible for this to be a conscious mind, but, since we have good reason to believe in functionalism, we shouldn't allow this intuition to undermine the view. Other functionalists take this challenge as a reason to restrict the input/output/interaction profile to neurally specified functions. If we specify inputs in terms of the optic nerve and outputs in terms of the motor cortices, then the nation of China won't count as a mind – its inputs and outputs won't be of the right kind. This risks undermining the multiple realization motivation by moving a more "chauvinistic" picture, but it avoids the problem of the China brain.

A final worry for functionalists is that even if we don't go in for zombies and China brains, we might worry that the functionalist views canvassed here fail to adequately distinguish between conscious and nonconscious states. A wide range of research in cognitive science shows that many of the things we formerly thought could only be done consciously can in fact be done nonconsciously. To the point, it may be that non-modular, integrative cognition can occur without consciousness. And this seems to undermine the initial functional definition motivating the GWS. Work by psychologists such as Timothy Wilson (2002) and Daniel Wegner (2003), among many others, shows that consciousness may be the small tip of a submerged, nonconscious iceberg, rather than a central integrative processing stage. Consciousness seems to be late arriving and confabulatory. Research shows that our subjective experience of events that we ourselves make happen occurs almost half a second *after* the brain initiates the action (Libet 1985; see also Haggard 2005). Our brains seem to decide what to do without us! What's more, the sense that we are the authors of various actions can be systematically misled by varying the timing and connection between events. However, consciously it seems to us that we did the thing, even if we didn't. It's like consciousness arrives a bit late, sees what's going on, and says "I did that!" To the extent that consciousness is not centrally involved in lots of what we do, the workspace idea loses traction. It may well be that the network does its thing unconsciously and then sends a signal out after the work is done to a kind of "press secretary." Consciousness may be the mouthpiece, rather than the executive.

What's more, it remains unclear how to tell which sorts of "skilled dancings" are conscious and which aren't. In fact, as any dancer knows, if you consciously attend to your dancing, that's just when you'll step on your partner's toes. It seems that the best dancing may be nonconscious! And to speak less metaphorically, we engage in a wide range of complex, skilled interactions with our environment. Some are conscious, some aren't. And some move back and forth between the two, depending on our focus. What's happening to account for the change? Even when we unconsciously interact with the environment, we still are poised to access the information we need – it seems as poised as in the conscious case. We don't have a clear way to make the crucial distinction here, between conscious and nonconscious states, even if we take the states to extend to body and world.

Functionalists, no doubt, have a range of responses to these claims. Mercifully, the responses tend to be empirical, rather than zombie-based. But the door seems open to a richer conception, one that retains the reductive aspirations of functionalism and respects the possibility of multiple realization, but moves beyond the basic functionalist framework. We'll look at two distinct versions of these *representationalist* views in the next two chapters.

Further Reading

A good starting point is Daniel Dennett's rich and provocative *Consciousness Explained*. Bernard Baars's *In the Theater of Consciousness* is a good introduction to the global workspace view. And see Alva Noë's 2005 *Action in Perception* for a look at the "enactive" approach. See Ned Block's important 1978 article "Troubles with Functionalism" for a good overview of functionalism, as well as some of the major criticisms of the view. For the more general functionalist approach to the mind, see Braddon-Mitchell and Jackson (2006), for a start.

7
First-Order Representationalism

Representationalist theories form a subset of functionalist theories.[1] Representationalism holds that consciousness can be explained as a kind of representing, as a special sort of informational tracking of the world or the self. If you do the right kind of representing, you are a conscious state. But this of course raises the question of just what it means to represent. And that may be as big a problem as a theory of consciousness! Some have worried that there just cannot be a naturalized theory of representation, so looking here for a reductive account of consciousness is a mistake. But over the last forty years or so, in both psychology and philosophy, a tentative consensus – or at least a mild optimism – has emerged concerning the prospects of a naturalized theory of representation. And if that is in the offing, the door is open to use such a theory to handle consciousness as well. Representation adds an intermediate step in the reduction of consciousness to brain. Instead of having to match neurons and conscious states, we can first reduce consciousness to representing and then, by using the naturalized theory we already have in hand, reduce representation to brain processes. An enticing prospect. But can it work? Two main lines of representational theory have been developed: "first-order" and "higher-order" representationalism. Again, I'll be using these terms rather broadly to capture a range of different views. Some theorists might resist the labels, but I'll make clear how

I see the theories fitting into one camp or the other. This chapter deals with first-order representationalism, the following one with the higher-order variety. And throughout, we'll see that representationalists often help themselves to functionalist ideas as well. So long as we end up at a strongly reductive picture, one that reductively explains consciousness as being this or that functional-representational process, all is well.

Theories of Representation

What, then, are representations? Representations are things that are *about* something else. There are lots of familiar examples of representations in our world. Pictures are representations. A picture of a cat is about a cat. Sentences are representations. "The cat is on the mat" represents the cat as being on the mat. That's what it's about. The words we speak are representations as well: when I say "Biscuit is friendly," I've said something about my dog Biscuit. Representations, in the sense that is of interest here, have a further very cool feature. They can be about things that don't exist, here, now, or ever. For example, I might talk about my pet lizard Joe, who, sadly, is no more. My words still are about Joe. Or a child might draw a picture of Santa Claus. Even though – spoiler alert! – Santa doesn't exist, the picture is still about Santa. Another way of putting all this, one that will be helpful for developing a naturalized theory of representation, is that representations *carry information* about the things they represent. The picture of the cat carries information about the cat. And so does the sentence. And, again, there's a decent sense in which the picture of Santa carries information about him as well – that he's got a beard, that he's got a jelly-like belly, and so on. Representations are items that carry information about other things, even things that don't exist. Philosophers sometimes use the slightly confusing term "intentionality" to pick out the property of representing. Representations, they say, display intentionality. Representational states are intentional states. But note that 'intentionality' here does not mean deliberate or voluntary! Rather, it's taken from the Latin word meaning "to point."

But it seems that the source of all representations may be us! We have conventions that make it the case that a series of ink squiggles *means* cat. There's nothing intrinsic to those lines of ink that do it. Rather, we know that those marks stand for sounds that match the spoken word for cat. But the sound CAT is no more intrinsically cat-like than the printed letters. The representational capacities of the sound CAT come from us. We've agreed (tacitly, no doubt) that in English, the sound CAT will pick out those devious, fuzzy guys. But how could we do this in the first place? The answer seems to be that our minds have the capacity to represent things and this comes first. We represent something mentally and then agree upon sounds and ink marks to convey those ideas. So we need to know how it is that our mental states could come to represent things, how they could ever display intentionality. And this, historically, has seemed a tough task to many philosophers. Things in the natural world, like atoms or brain states, can only be causally connected. The big trick is to figure out how we might build a theory of representations out of causal parts. But A being caused by B is generally not enough for A to represent B. Here's why. It might be that cats are the normal cause of a certain mental state in me. We might want to say that the state represents cats. But every now and then, perhaps very rarely, the state is caused by small dogs on dark nights. So, does my state really mean "cat or small dog on dark nights"? We need a way to say that the state is sometimes *misrepresenting*. We want to say: no, when the dogs trigger the state, that is an error. It still means cat. So what we really need is a way to explain misrepresentation. If we can do that using only natural ingredients, we'll be on our way. This is the "problem of naturalizing intentionality."

How might it be that our mental states cannot only causally co-vary with things in the world, but in addition actually represent them? A number of naturalist proposals have been developed, starting with the informational approach of Fred Dretske (1981; 1995).[2] He argued that items in the natural world come to represent by having the *function* to represent. And they get this function either by evolution or by learning.

There may be a state in a primitive creature that happens to co-vary with the presence of oxygen. If the creature can come to exploit this information in a way conducive to its goals, then the state will acquire the function of representing oxygen. Perhaps a mutation allows this information to be exploited. Some new structure in the creature reacts to the presence of the state co-varying with oxygen (perhaps by triggering a move), and it leads to the evolutionary success of the creature vs. its rivals. An example of such a creature might be a simple bacterium having membranes sensitive to oxygen. When those membranes react, the creature wriggles wildly, causing it to move away from its current location. In this way, an anaerobic bacterium may come to have states that have the function of detecting oxygen, rather than merely causally co-varying with it. We have the rudimentary beginnings of representation.

We can then build on this basic foundation, adding in learning mechanisms, systems that are built to exploit new information as it comes in and to associate it with things that matter to a critter. These sorts of classical conditioning mechanisms allow us to create new and meaningful representations of our environment. In a learning situation, a co-varying item can acquire the function of representing something else. For example, if a critter can detect the co-occurrence of a bell and food, then it can learn that the bell *indicates* or *means* food. The learning phase pins down the correct target of the representation, greatly expanding the range of what we can represent. And as we acquire more and more sophisticated cognitive abilities, we can come to calibrate our representations with extremely abstract and subtle things in the world. And once we have the power to misrepresent, we can represent in the absence of the representations target. We can represent a thing that is not there. But what about things that are *never* there, like Santa? Here, we might build complex representations out of simpler parts. We have a representation or the real things red, fat, beard, jolly, and so on, and we put them together to form a representation of a fellow who doesn't exist. With a store of basic parts and the ability to misrepresent, we seem to have reached all we need for a theory of intentionality.

I've given a rather impressionistic version of Dretske's mature theory, but, even when all the details are laid out, it remains controversial. Can evolution and learning really explain the hyper-precision with which we can represent? How could evolution ever cut things so finely? And is it really possible to build all the nonexistent and fictional things we muse over out of a stock of basic causally grounded bits? Can we really represent things as abstract as justice or freedom that way?[3] For our purposes, I will allow that there is a workable naturalized theory of representation for the taking. It seems to me that we have a better grip on how such a theory might go than we do about how a theory of consciousness might go; so if we can reduce consciousness to representation, we've made some progress, even if there are still outstanding issues. It may be that, in the end, the two problems will collapse into one, that of explaining *conscious representing*, rather than whatever it is that simple animals or perhaps computers do. But it's worth seeing if we can keep the issues separate, to discover how far we can get.

It's also worth noting that there is another way to naturalize intentionality, one that is closer to the functionalist camp. It holds that to represent something is to play the right *functional role* in a creature. A state represents cats, say, if it is reliably caused by cats, interacts in the right way with other thoughts (animal thoughts, pet thoughts, etc.) and it causes the appropriate cat-directed behavior. This may or may not require us to bring in information and evolutionary function.[4] Or it may be that a blended view, using both functional role and informational tracking, is the right view. Again, so long as we can reduce, it works for the purposes of a strongly reductive theory of consciousness.

Transparency and "Standard" First-Order Representationalism

Given a naturalized theory of representation, what can we now say about consciousness? At first blush, this is again barking up the wrong tree. Representations explain, perhaps, what it means to have beliefs, desires, goals, and so forth – what philosophers call "propositional attitude" states, states where the subject "takes an attitude," like believing or desiring, towards a proposition, like "Paris is in France." To explain people's propositional attitudes, we can hold that they have states representing the world and they then take attitudes, spelled out in functional terms, towards the content of these representations. There is much debate about just how to spell this all out, but it does seem to be a promising research program. But the theoretical approach is most promising exactly when we leave out consciousness, when we *don't* have to say anything about what it's like, how it *feels* to believe or desire such-and-such, and so on. We just explain what it means for a person to believe that Paris is in France without having to wade into the morass of consciousness studies. But representational theories of consciousness, of course, dive in head first! What could motivate this move?

The main factor motivating representationalism, at least in its main form, is the perceptual phenomenon known as *transparency*. Transparency, according to representationalists, is the claim that when we introspect on our perceptual mental states, we never find anything *mental*! All we find are things in the world, generally three-dimensional colored objects viewed from a particular point of view (at least in the visual domain). When we introspect, we don't become aware of our mental states; rather, we become aware, in a focused and attentive way, of what those mental states tell us about the world. That is, we become aware of what those mental states *represent*. Philosopher Gil Harman, a proponent of representationalism, puts it like this:

> What Eloise sees before her is a tree, whether or not it is a hallucination. That is to say, the content of her visual experience is that she is presented with a tree, not with an idea of a tree. Perhaps, Eloise's visual experience involves some sort of mental picture of the environment. It does not follow that she is aware of a mental picture. If there is a mental picture, it may be that what she is aware of is whatever is represented by that mental picture; but then that mental picture represents something in the world, not something in the mind. (Harman 1990: 36)

We become aware of the tree and its bark, not special qualitative properties of our mental states. And this suggests that what's going on when we have conscious perceptual experiences is that we represent the world as being this way or that. At least prima facie, we don't need to posit any special inner "mental paint" or intrinsic qualia when we theorize about consciousness. All we need is representations of the right sort. This is the task of a theory of consciousness: to explain the right sorts of representations involved in consciousness and to explain why these representations are conscious rather than nonconscious.

The two main philosophers who've most taken the message of transparency to heart are Fred Dretske (1995) and Michael Tye (1995, 2000). Both have developed theories of consciousness where the key element is a specific kind of representation, a representation about properties in the world. When these representations play the right functional roles, they are conscious. Because the representations are of the world, rather than about other representations of the subject, we call them "first-order representations," in contrast to "higher-order representations." Dretske and Tye defend "first-order representational" theories of consciousness, or "FOR" theories. (The acronyms for theories of consciousness will get pretty thick from here on out, but it does save time in typing!)

Dretske's and Tye's theories are very similar, both in spirit and letter. Both accept what is known as "strong transparency," the claim that we're *never* directly aware of our mental states, even in introspection; rather, we're only aware of the properties those mental states represent. Weaker versions of transparency hold that, though we're usually only aware of what our mental states represent, at times we can be directly aware of the mental states and their properties. "Directly" is added to remove any roundabout indirect way we might be aware of our mental states by first being aware of something else.

Both theorists also hold that the *content* of consciousness – what we're aware *of* in conscious experience – shows that the representations accounting for consciousness must be "nonconceptual." That is, the representations must be more detailed and fine-grained than anything we have words for or that we can cognitively categorize and recall in thought. The idea here is that conscious seeing provides us with much more detail than we can process cognitively, but that detail is still present to us in experience. A metaphoric way to capture this is to say that the "picture" of consciousness is worth a thousand cognitive "words." For example, when you look at a complex visual scene, like a busy city street, you see much more detail than you can "put into mental words." Or when you look at the colorful swirl of a figurine done in Venetian glass, you can see an incredible blending of colors and shapes, even though you have no specific concepts for those colors and shapes and couldn't recognize them in isolation. Still, we consciously see them. So, conclude Dretske and Tye, our visual experience must be produced by *nonconceptual* representations. Finally, they agree that the key transition making these nonconceptual representations conscious is that they are "poised" at the doorway to our conceptual systems. They serve as the perceptual input to cognition. But if the representations are not available in this way, they are not conscious states. Thus, we get a functionalist way of separating out the conscious from the nonconscious representations.

Dretske's specific way of putting things (1995) is that there is a special class of mental representations that are built into an organism at the get-go. These representations are the ground-level representations of a system, constructed by evolution to track key properties in a creature's world. Dretske calls these "systematic" representations. They are nonconceptual, as noted, so they can be possessed by simple critters lacking our rich conceptual abilities. Dretske suggests we consider a frog looking at a poodle. The frog can certainly see the poodle, as can we. But the frog can't see the poodle *as* a poodle. Only we, with our concept of POODLE, can do so. Still, there is plausibly some level of representation we share with the frog when looking at the poodle and this is of the nonconceptual systematic sort. Dretske has also written of these kinds of representations having "analog" content, in contrast to the "digital" representations of concepts (1981). Dretske goes on to say that these representations serve as input to our conceptual systems and they only become conscious at this point. One wonders if the frog's representations are not conscious at all for that reason, but perhaps he has simple froggy concepts. All of this is meant to be ultimately reducible to physical processes. Dretske, as noted above, is one of the major proponents of a naturalized theory of representation and argues that we can explain the representations constituting consciousness in those terms. Thus we get a full-blown strong reduction. Consciousness is representation of the right sort, and representation is a causal process of the right sort, involving our brains and the world we live in. That's all there is to it.

Tye's (1995) view shares these main features. He also calls for nonconceptual representation and in support offers that while we can consciously see the difference between very close-by shades of a color, we generally cannot tell which was which when later presented with just one of them. This indicates, according to Tye, that we can see more than we can conceptualize because concepts are implicated in the process of remembering and reidentifying things at later times. Tye endorses a similar sort of informational tracking theory of representation, holding that a state represents its target when it stands in the right causal relationship, one selected for by evolution. Again, a state represents what it was selected to represent, allowing for the crucial explanation of the possibility of misrepresentation. And Tye agrees that conscious representations must be properly "poised" to influence the conceptual belief-desire systems. Tye points out that blindsight subjects (see p. 74) might have the right sorts of nonconceptual representations, but those representations are not properly poised to influence their belief-desire systems, rendering them unconscious.[5] Dretske's and Tye's views are quite close, as we can see, though they do differ in some fine details beyond the scope of our discussion here.

It is also crucial to note that FOR theory is not just about visual consciousness. It is meant to apply to conscious experience in *all* the sensory modalities. Again, the view holds that we have nonconceptual auditory, tactile, and even olfactory and gustatory representations, and when these are properly poised to influence our conceptual systems, we become conscious of what the representations represent. But what might these representations be tracking? FOR holds that auditory representations track things like car horns, electric guitars, and slamming doors. Or more precisely, they track the acoustic properties underlying these things (remember, even frogs, who know little of electric guitars, can hear them!). And so it goes for the other modalities: we track the real properties in the world causing our experiences, like colors, sounds, smells, and tastes. Note that this requires that there really are such things out there in the world to be tracked! Because of their adherence to strong transparency and an informational tracking view of representation, FOR can't appeal to any inner qualities to "color" our experience. It must all be out there, at least some of the time, so our representations can properly latch on to their targets. Many have felt this is a serious worry – what things are the real colors out there in the world, for example? Aren't colors more about how we react to energy or wavelengths of light or whatever? This issue, about *realism* for color and other "sensory qualities" is a serious issue in metaphysics. We can't go into the many ins and outs of that debate, but we can at least note that the FOR theory takes on this burden and cannot remain neutral in that metaphysical battle-royal.

But what of features of our experience that don't plausibly seem "out there" at all, like emotions, moods, and bodily states like pleasure and pain? Even those can be given a representational treatment, according to proponents of FOR. Emotions might represent the states of our bodies or states of the world, and pains represent damage to specific bodily locations. A good mood might represent the world in general in a positive way. And so on. These claims are considerably less intuitive than the claims about transparent awareness of visual properties, but perhaps if the theory is successful in the prominent cases of vision and audition, it gives us reason to allow for a less intuitive gloss of pleasures, pains, and moods. It is often the case that a successful theory requires us to give up some of our pre-theoretical intuitions – see relativity and quantum mechanics, for example! So FOR may well be able to capture the range of conscious qualities. And what of conscious thoughts or desires? Of conscious musings and theorizing? What is being tracked in these cases? Here, the FOR can hold that the only properties conscious in cognitive processing are the sensory representations used in perception. Perhaps when we muse about justice, we get a visual image of a scale or the auditory experience of a gavel banging. Those can be accounted for in terms of perceptual representations. But it's not clear that there's really anything else to conscious cognition if we strip away *all* the accompanying sensory imagery. Thus, it may be that there's nothing the FOR needs to account for here. The question of "cognitive phenomenology" is a difficult one, plaguing psychology from the late 1800s. The issue is still a live one and it is far from being settled by psychologists or philosophers. Again, the FOR is committed to one side of the debate, but that just means it might be empirically falsifiable, like a good empirical theory should be.

Thus we are left with a relatively straightforward reductive theory of consciousness, one respecting many of our intuitions about the sorts of things we experience, while also providing a route to strong reduction. Further, the view blends well with the main body of research in cognitive science, with its embrace of information processing. Finally, the view avoids the need to posit mysterious inner "qualia" – those glowing mental gumdrops of doom. Qualia are represented by our mental states. They are the colors, shapes, sounds, tastes, and so on out there in the world that we consciously come into contact with in experience. If this element of FOR can be made to work, one of the major stumbling blocks to a theory of consciousness falls. We'll consider general objections to the view at the end of the chapter. (Spoiler alert: not everyone is convinced!) But first, we'll consider a somewhat different representational theory, one not too far from FOR, but rejecting strong transparency. Also, the view provides a much stronger functionalist component, relying on *attention* to separate conscious from nonconscious representations. The view is Jesse Prinz's "attended, intermediate representation," or AIR, theory. (I warned you that we're entering heavy acronym territory!)

Prinz's AIR Theory[6]

Prinz's AIR theory (2012) is a piece of "neurophilosophy" – philosophy deeply shaped by our most current knowledge of the brain. In this, he's not far from Patricia Churchland or some of the identity theorists we met, but among the representationalists we'll consider, he's the most brain-focused. He rejects the central plank of the standard FOR view, holding

⇀ that strong transparency is not correct. There is good reason, he contends, to hold that our representations of the world "color" what we see and that much of what we experience is a projection of features we wrongly take to be in the world. But, despite this difference, he is strongly committed to the idea that we are conscious of what our brains represent, and figuring out just how this works is key to a theory of consciousness. Prinz considers the question of the level of detail present in conscious experience. Are we aware of extremely "low-level" features, like light gradients and color boundaries? Are we aware of abstract "high-level" features like the gradual ending of an economic recession? No, we are aware of what Prinz terms "intermediate" representations, those picking out mid-sized objects and everyday properties. There is a sort of "Goldilocks' principle" when it comes to conscious representations: not too detailed and not too abstract. Intermediate representations are "just right!" Prinz bases this claim in part on phenomenological reflection. This is just what we find when we consider what we're conscious of. And for Prinz, a crucial feature of being intermediate is that the information represented is given from a "point of view." It is integrated into our map of where we are in the world. Low-level information lacks this integration and high-level features abstract away from it. But Prinz also appeals to data from the cognitive science of vision to support the importance of the intermediate level. A famous theory in that domain, David Marr's computational theory of vision (1982), holds that conscious visual experience employs a "2½-D" sketch, poised in between lower and higher levels of processing. Also, Prinz leans on the work of cognitive scientist Ray Jackendoff (1987), who argues for the centrality of intermediate-level processing. Finally, Prinz considers what brain areas are most highly correlated with conscious experience. He contends that, once again, we find that intermediate-level processing, between the lower-level sensory cortices and the higher-level frontal processes, seems the best candidate for the neural correlate of consciousness. Taken together, Prinz holds that this makes a strong case for intermediate-level representations, one not simply based on philosophical intuitions, but taking into account phenomenological and empirical data.

I have placed Prinz's view in this chapter as it shares some key features with FOR theory. Most fundamentally, the theoretical approach is to identify the right sort of representational content involved in consciousness, and then offer a route to reduction by appeal to a naturalized theory of representation. Prinz offers such a naturalized view, one taking on a number of pieces of the Dretske-style informational tracking picture, but leavening it with other elements. The details of this interesting approach would take us too far afield, but, like Dretske's and Tye's, Prinz's view seems well-placed to offer a strongly reductive explanation of consciousness. However, at key points in defending his view, Prinz retreats to a more local and limited reductive account, holding that the best we can do is identify consciousness in *us* with attended intermediate-level representations, leaving grander metaphysical questions about the *essence* of consciousness, zombies, and so on for another time. In this, again, his view resembles other neurophilosophers, who tend to beg off the larger questions as being beyond the scope of science. Still, one can imagine an extended version of Prinz's theory being offered to cover all consciousness, claiming that to be conscious is just to have attended intermediate-level representations. At times in the objections section, I'll consider this "post-Prinz" version of the AIR theory.

But so far, we just have the "IR." What about the "A"? Prinz acknowledges that being an intermediate-level representation isn't enough to make a state conscious. An additional factor is needed. According to Prinz, only *attended* intermediate-level representations are conscious. Again, Prinz appeals to both phenomenological and empirical factors to make his case. There does seem to be something to the fact that if a representation is completely unattended, it isn't conscious. This intuitive point receives support from a range of psychological research. "Inattentional blindness" occurs when we "miss" things right in front of us because we are focused on a task (Mack and Rock 1989). A famous (and "viral") example is Daniel Simons's "gorillas in our midst" study (Chabris and Simons 2009).[7] Subjects are asked to count the successful passes of the basketball by one team as they're being defended by another. The players swirl around in weaving patterns and it takes some effort to keep track.

At the end of the task, a question is asked: "Did you see the gorilla?" Many (myself included!) think, "What in the world are you talking about?" But then the video is replayed, this time with explicit instructions to look for the gorilla. A person in a goofy-looking gorilla suit walks in front of the basketball players, hits his chest and strides off. I thought it was a new video, but it isn't. Attending to the passing game rendered me "blind" to even an obvious and centrally located stimulus. This phenomenon has been repeated in many experiments. Prinz uses it to support that idea that unattended representations are not conscious. We see the same thing in a range of different studies in psychology and in certain neurological phenomena too. Prinz concludes that attention is necessary for consciousness. What's more, if intermediate-level representations are the focus of attention, it is sufficient for consciousness as well.

But, what, exactly, *is* attention? One worry is that all the hard stuff has now been moved over to a theory of attention, with its special consciousness-conferring powers. Further, in the psychological and neurological literature, there is a large range of processes going by the name of attention. Some are relatively low-level and "early," and so seem ill-suited for a key role in consciousness. Others are top-down and voluntary, but perhaps too high-level and intermittent to account for our everyday experience. Prinz tries to avoid these issues by defining attention in terms of working memory. In his view "attention can be identified with the processes that allow information to be encoded in working memory" (2012: 93). Attention moves intermediate representational content into a memory system where it can be used for "executive control." Again, we see a functional component being added to the initial representational element. When this occurs, the intermediate-level content becomes conscious. And again, as with the global workspace, we see that working memory is a key functional element in consciousness. Intermediateness tells us what is conscious and attention tells us how it becomes conscious (Mole 2013). Prinz provides a great deal of neurological evidence that damage to working memory systems undermines consciousness and that those areas best correlated with consciousness include the working memory systems. Of course, it is also true that those areas are best correlated with our *reports* of consciousness, so it remains possible that consciousness and working memory might come apart. But from the neurophilosophical perspective, it would seem that working memory is deeply intertwined with consciousness.

Thus, we get another sort of theory where consciousness occurs when the right sort of representational content – what a representation tells us – is processed in the appropriate way. And again we see the relatively short step from such a theory to a brain-based reduction of consciousness. Ultimately, the representational/functional features accounting for consciousness can be understood in terms of the firing patterns of neurons. Indeed, Prinz goes so far as to offer a neurological version of his proposal, invoking what are known as "gamma-band" oscillations to explain how intermediate-level representations become available to working memory. When patterns of neural firings occur in the right regions and when they synchronize around the 40 MHz range, they are available to working memory. We've reached a brain-level theory of consciousness, one alive to phenomenological and empirical data. And it has a catchy acronym. What more do you want from us?

Worries for FOR

One key worry about FOR theory is getting the representations right. The same thing can be represented in lots of ways. I can represent a cat by saying 'cat,' by drawing a picture of a cat, by developing a theory of the cat, and so on. And even when it comes to mental representation, there seems to be more than one way to represent the same thing. I can think about a cat, for example by thinking "the cat is on the mat." But I can also *see* the cat and have a "perceptual image" of it. What is the nature of this kind of representation? Both Dretske and Tye hold that this sort of representation is "non-conceptual." But that does not tell us enough. That is to say that it isn't the same kind of representation as when I think "the cat is on the mat." But what is it? There seems to be something imagistic or picture-like going on. But how do we characterize this without reference to "mental paint," the coloring features of mental states themselves? This is a serious problem for adherents to strong transparency, like Dretske and Tye. But even if, like Prinz, we reject strong transparency, we cannot help ourselves to qualia, the intrinsic, irreducible qualitative features of mental states, to explain conscious representation, at least not if we want to retain some degree of reductive explanation.

One move is to say that, while conceptual representations pick out broad categories like cats or dogs, perceptual representations track more basic detectable features like color, shape, texture, and so on. These can be combined in rich ways to give us what we consciously perceive. We build complex visual objects, for examples, out of a range of represented sensory primitives. But this doesn't seem to tell us enough, again. I can conceptually pick out those basic features as well, as I do in a psychological theory. A scientific theory representing the fine-grained low-level features of reality we perceive will not, on the FOR theory, provide us with a conscious perceptual experience of those things. So the *features* we represent can't make the distinction we want. It's something more. And Dretske's appeal to "systematic" representations likewise is uninformative. Why should it matter that the representations are "built in" by evolution? What we want to know is what it is about these built-in representations that provides us with the particular qualities we experience in conscious perception.

And there is a further pressing worry for representationalists like Dretske and Tye who appeal to an informational tracking theory of representation, one that explains what we see strictly by appeal to what we represent in the world and not by reference to the features of the representations doing that work. Our sensory modalities display a pattern of similarities and differences. Red is more similar to purple than it is to green. A trumpet sounds more like a trombone than it does a piano. And so forth. Indeed, a range of psychophysical research establishes how these similarities and differences are related in what's known as a *quality space* (Clark 1993). A quality space lays out the similarities and differences in a sensory modality, mapping all the dimensions along which the stimuli in a modality can vary. Think about the so-called "color solid," displaying the interrelations between all the colors we see. Similar "spaces" can be generated to sounds, tastes, and the other modalities. But why should this cause a problem for informational tracking views? There seems to be nothing in the represented features themselves explaining the similarity and differences we see, for example. We see the colors as forming a "wheel," where we run from red to orange to yellow to green to blue to purple and back to red. But in nature we find a color "line" with red at one end and blue at the other. It seems that the best explanation of the circle is the contribution of our sensory apparatus to what we see. And that undermines the kind of transparent realism entailed by the traditional FOR approach. Prinz's rejection of strong transparency allows him to appeal to internal features of representations to explain these connections. But differentiating just the right sort of representation remains a pressing difficulty for the representationalist approach.

And then there is the question, touched on briefly above, of nonrepresentational experiences. Do pains really represent something? Or do they just hurt? And what does my free-floating joyous mood track? Somewhat embarrassingly, the philosophical debate on this matter has focused on the experience of orgasm. Certainly this is a very distinct conscious experience! But does it really represent something? Representationalists have contended that the experience represents "voiding" and "pleasure down there" and so on. Perhaps. But is that all there is to it? Another problem case is the "phosphenes" we can experience by pressing on our closed eyelids. We experience a range of floating colorful spots – are they really representing something else? Representationalists reply that indeed, what we're experiencing is colorful spots out there in front of us, even though we know that the representations are non-veridical. It seems to me that for every purported nonrepresentational feature of experience, there is a not completely implausible response. This debate seems to be a push: no clear winner emerges. But some may find one side or the other compelling. Note again that this is only a challenge to holders of strong transparency.

A final worry about FOR is that it falls into the same problems as the more basic forms of functionalism. Indeed, one can argue that there really isn't much space at all between functionalism and FOR theory. What's doing the crucial work of making a state conscious is availability to conceptualization or working memory, not the fact that something is represented. And these are straightforwardly functional notions. So, one pressing question we can ask is do these theories really pick out the right functional features to account for the difference between conscious and nonconscious representations? It appears that there can be low-level representations not only available to but actively conceptualized that nonetheless remain nonconscious. In studies of subliminal priming – the quick flashing of stimuli to subjects below the threshold of awareness – there are cases where only conceptualization can explain the results (Merikle, Smilek, and Eastwood 2001). But this seems to undermine the traditional FOR picture. In such cases, we have lower-level representations, as the theory dictates, and they are available to higher-level cognition (indeed, they've been taken up by the conceptual system). Still, they aren't conscious, in contrast to what the theory dictates. FOR theorists can refine their claims about just what the representations are available to. Perhaps a blending with the global workspace view would be helpful here. But again, we see that it's the workspace, rather than the representations, doing the key work here. It may be that FOR theorists never meant to be explaining anything beyond what the *content* of consciousness is, rather than a theory of how contents become conscious. If so, the theory loses considerable scope.

And it's not fully clear that the traditional FOR theories get the content right, either. Is it really so obvious that only nonconceptual content is conscious? Are we never aware of things as we conceptualize them? One way to think about this question is to consider what happens to experience when we learn new concepts.[8] On the FOR view, nothing happens, at least not directly. The nonconceptual content determines what it's like for us, and the concepts determine how we classify things cognitively. But an alternative view of what happens when we learn to appreciate classical music or we learn to taste fine wine is that our concepts actively alter how things seem to us directly. Now that we know about oboes, we can actually *hear* them in the music. The FOR theorist can respond that concepts *cause* changes in our lower-level nonconceptual representations, rather than directly contributing to what it's like for us. Again, the FOR view takes a strong stand on what seems to be an open issue.

Finally, we haven't really vanquished the zombies. If they're still roaming the landscape, it's fair to ask if it's really inconceivable that a creature with the right first-order representations might lack consciousness. Is that guaranteed or entailed by the FOR view? Perhaps we should just give up on worrying about zombies, but, if that's the problem driving us, it's not clear that FOR has anything more to say than functionalism. We remain in search of a view that both scratches the zombie itch *and* provides a reasonable route to reduction. Perhaps we just can't have both. But the theories reviewed in the final chapter – "higher-order" and "self-representational" approaches – hope to enrich the functional-representational view enough to shut the door on the walking undead. We'll see.

Further Reading

The key texts for FOR view are Harman's "The Intrinsic Quality of Experience," Dretske's *Naturalizing the Mind*, and Tye's *Ten Problems of Consciousness*. Tye's later *Consciousness, Color, and Content* defends and expands the view. An important criticism not discussed in this book is Ned Block's "Inverted Earth" (1990). See also Carruthers (2000), ch. 6; and Gennaro (2012), ch. 3, for further criticisms. Prinz's AIR theory is defended in his 2012 *The Conscious Brain: How Attention Engenders Experience*.

8
Higher-Order Representationalism

The final group of theories we'll look at I'll broadly label "higher-order" representational views. All the theories of this type hold that mental states are conscious when the subject is appropriately *conscious of* being in them. It may seem at the outset that the views can only offer a circular explanation, one explaining consciousness in terms of consciousness. Not very informative! But higher-order views stress a key distinction between a mental state being conscious, full stop, and a subject being conscious *of* something. This second thing, labeled "transitive consciousness" by higher-order theorist David Rosenthal, can plausibly be explained in terms of representation (Rosenthal 1986; 2005). So we explain what it is for a mental state to be conscious ("intransitive" consciousness) in terms of representing, which makes us conscious of the state (transitive consciousness). So, assuming we can make good an explanation of transitive consciousness in reductive representational terms, circularity is avoided. We'll say more about this way of thinking about consciousness in a moment.

There are three main types of higher-order views we'll look at here. First is the traditional "extrinsic" higher-order approach, cast either in terms of higher-order thoughts or higher-order perceptions, views defended by Rosenthal, David Armstrong, and William Lycan, among others.[1] The second approach is the "self-representational" theory, defended recently by Uriah Kriegel and Rocco Gennaro, but having its roots in a long history of philosophical theorizing, particularly in the phenomenological tradition.[2] The last view we'll look at is something of a hybrid approach, defended by Robert Van Gulick.[3] His view takes elements of the higher-order approach but also looks to functionalism and the global workspace in particular for inspiration. I'll close, as usual, by considering the main objections to the view.

The Transitivity Principle

The higher-order representational approach is rooted in a particular way of looking at consciousness. We are asked to consider what makes the difference between states that are conscious and those that are not. This, of course, assumes that at least some mental states can occur nonconsciously, but this is now a widely accepted idea in both philosophy and science (though, recall that it wasn't always. Descartes, among others, rejected it). What then is the difference between conscious and nonconscious states, in everyday terms? Higher-order theorists note that if we're in no way aware of (or conscious of – I'll use these two interchangeably here) a mental state, intuitively this isn't a conscious state. But if states we're in no way aware of are not conscious states, it follows that conscious states are states we're in some way aware of. This gives us a nice way to characterize conscious states. So far, it's only a rough commonsense claim. It may not bear much weight or do much to differentiate between various views. But it does provide a useful way to orient oneself, rather than focusing on "what it's like for a subject," which seems to tilt towards an isolated, subjective way of putting things. This idea – that conscious states are states we're aware of – is called the "transitivity principle" by Rosenthal (2005). All higher-order views take the transitivity principle as a jumping-off point, even if they later diverge greatly.

But what more can be said in support of this idea? And what are its implications for a theory of consciousness? A range of empirical results can be interpreted as giving support to the transitivity idea, some of which we've already met in other chapters. For example, so-called "inattentional blindness," considered in the last chapter, suggests that if we aren't aware of a stimulus, because we're distracted by a task, say, then it won't be conscious. And there is further evidence, from phenomena like "masked priming" where quickly flashed stimuli are occluded by a following mask, that information gets into the mind and is represented, even though that information remains unconscious.[4] One way to interpret this is that the information is there, but we're not aware of it, in keeping with the transitivity principle. And it may be that damage in cases like "blindsight" (see chapter 5, Block's distinction between "access" and "phenomenal" consciousness) are examples of information that's in us, but of which we're unaware. All of these sorts of cases can be given other theoretical glosses, but they fit nicely with the transitivity principle. The principle thus comports well with empirical data, as well as capturing at least something of our common-sense notion of consciousness.

But how do we move from the transitivity principle to the higher-order approach? The higher-order approach takes the primary task of a theory of consciousness to be one of explaining how the transitivity principle is realized in us. Other questions and puzzles concerning consciousness are then to be taken up in light of whatever theoretical framework we come up with to handle transitivity. And while many of the major proponents of the higher-order approach are in the strongly reductive camp (all the ones we'll look at in this chapter fit this mold), there are also nonreductive versions of the theory, both historical and contemporary.[5] So a theory explaining the transitivity principle need not be reductive, though the possibility of a reductive version is one of the major attractions for many of its supporters.

As a first step in developing a theory, we must pick out just what kind of awareness we're looking for. Not every way of being aware of one's mental states makes them conscious. For instance, if someone tells me I'm in a particular mental state and I believe them, that's a way to become aware of my own state. But it isn't enough to make the state conscious. My awareness has to be "direct" in some sense. It must not seem that there's anything mediating between me and my conscious state. I must be aware of it without any inference or theory, or at least without any inference or theory I'm conscious of. And I also must be aware of the state *as mine*. It's not enough simply to be aware that a mental state is occurring. I might become aware of *your* mental state, perhaps in a very direct and spontaneous way, but that will not make it a conscious state. We have to be aware of our conscious states as our own. A way to put all this is that a mental state is conscious when I'm aware of myself as being in it in a suitably immediate way. This gives us a refined version of the transitivity principle. It also introduces a notion of *self-awareness* into the basic idea of consciousness. This is a move broadly accepted in the "phenomenological" tradition of Brentano, Husserl, Heidegger, and others.[6] It has its antecedents in Kant's work, among others. It is a controversial view and may actually be separable from a more basic transitive view where awareness of a state without reference to the self is enough to make the state conscious. But many of the main versions of the approach accept the self-element, so we'll stick to that.

How do we get to the standard higher-order representational view, then? Armstrong, Rosenthal, and Lycan have all argued that the best way to explain the transitivity principle is in representational terms. Representations, they contend, make us *conscious of* things. So it makes sense to posit representations accounting for the awareness we have of our conscious states. And, as we saw in the previous chapter, it's widely held that representation, in turn, can be given a reductive, functional explanation in terms of the workings of neural states. What sorts of representations should we be looking for, then? Representations that pick out other representations – representations that make us aware of our mental states. Hence the label "higher-order" representationalism. Armstrong and Lycan argue that the best model for the sort of representation making us aware of our conscious state is *perceptual* representation. Rosenthal argues that *thought* is a better fit. But all three agree that a separate, inner-directed representational state best accounts for the transitivity principle. We'll consider these views in a moment. The other main class of higher-order theory holds there is just one representation making us conscious of both the world and that state itself. Conscious states, on this view, are complex states with world-directed and self-directed elements. In essence, we have the two separate bits of the traditional higher-order view fused together into one complex state pointing both inside and out. According to the defenders of this approach, these self-representational structures have distinct theoretical advantages over the two-state approach. We'll consider that down the road. For now, we can see that both versions of the higher-order approach agree that the transitivity principle is best explained by positing inner-directed representational elements, and that ultimately these elements can be cashed out in physical terms.

The Traditional Higher-Order Approach

The traditional higher-order representation account holds that we become aware of a conscious state by forming a representation directed at it. This representation tells the subject, in essence, that she is in that very mental state, a state with such-and-such features. For example, to have a conscious experience of a red ball, the subject first forms a "first-order" representation of the ball, carrying the information that it's red, round, rubbery, and so on. That representation, as of yet, is nonconscious. Then she forms a higher-order representation to the effect that "I am seeing a round, red, rubbery ball, off to my left, under a table, etc." Note that the representation picks out the subject, the subject's mental state ("seeing") and describes the content of that state. Of course, the representation isn't in English; we're just using the language to capture what the state represents. Exactly *how* the state does represent is a matter of debate. But before we dive into that, there's another worry of a regress. If I have a representation describing myself as being in this or that state, doesn't it have to be conscious? And then we need a yet higher-order state to pick it out. But then the same problem repeats at the higher level, and we're off on an infinite regress. This is indeed a problem if one holds that all mental states are conscious. The early-modern philosopher John Locke held that and also held a version of the higher-order approach (Locke 1979 [1689]). He was attacked for this by the philosopher Gottfried Leibniz, Locke's contemporary (Leibniz 1989 [1714]). Leibniz held that there must be an unconscious mental state at the top of the chain in order to block the regress. And contemporary defenders of the traditional higher-order view agree. The higher-order state making us aware of our conscious state is itself *nonconscious*. This blocks the regress but raises serious questions about how the presence of a nonconscious state accounts for experience. We'll take that up in the objections section.

So a mental state becomes conscious, on this view, when a nonconscious representation of that state is formed. But the higher-order state must come about in the right way. It can't be formed as a result of any inference or process of which the subject is aware. It must seem to be formed non-inferentially, from the subject's point of view. This gives the subject a seemingly direct and unmediated awareness of her conscious state. Exactly how to cash out this immediacy requirement is a also matter of debate. Perhaps the higher-order state must be appropriately caused by the lower-order state it targets. Or maybe it is enough that it seems to the subject that there is no mediation, however the state comes about. What matters is the appearance of immediacy, not necessarily an actual lack of mediation. So long as the mediating factors occur "behind the scenes" the higher-order approach should get things right.

But what is the nature of the higher-order representation? Is it so special that it recreates the problems and mysteries at a higher level? The main defenders of the higher-order theory all argue that higher-order representation can be explained in fully reductive terms, leaving no residual mystery. The view as they conceive it is strongly reductive. David Armstrong and William Lycan argue that the higher-order representation is best modeled on perceptual processes. Their view, accordingly, is known as the "higher-order perception" (HOP) theory. HOP holds that the processes making us aware of our conscious states have certain features analogous to perception. For one, they work by a kind of scanning process. Our higher-order awareness tracks and picks out pertinent lower-level information to make conscious. This is similar to the way perceptual processes track and capture pertinent information in our nearby environment. Further, in conscious experience we are aware of a broad range of fine-grained sensory information. This seems to go beyond what we have concepts for (see the claims of FOR theory in the last chapter). And this, too, seems to be perception-like. It seems we can perceive more than we can categorize and label, so it is plausible that our higher-order awareness is best modeled on perception. Finally, perception is something often not under our control – it is triggered by noteworthy features of the environment, like the presence of a tiger. And what we're conscious of is likewise often out of our control. Things just "flow" in our stream of consciousness. We don't decide to be conscious of this or that mental state. Again, it seems like the sort of awareness we have of our conscious states resembles perception. What's more, both Armstrong and Lycan argue that perception can be cashed out in functional-representational terms. So it provides a good model for a reductive theory. The higher-order awareness is perception-like, perception is just functional-informational tracking, and so higher-order awareness can be captured in a functional-representational analysis.

David Rosenthal, on the other hand, rejects the perception model and argues for a "higher-order thought" (HOT) theory. Rosenthal contends that the key difference between perceiving and thinking is that perceiving involves sensory quality. When I perceive red, as opposed to merely thinking about red, I am aware of the redness of the perception. There is something sensory occurring, however we make sense of that. But these sensory qualities – the redness of a perceived apple or the shrillness of a heard trumpet – are plausibly features of first-order representations, representations tracking attributes of the world. But if higher-order states are to be perception-like, we need a story about *their* sensory qualities. But what could these be? Some higher-order quality tracking first-order redness? It's hard to see what the HOP theorist could appeal to in explaining these special new qualities. So Rosenthal concludes that the higher-order states themselves must not have a special sensory quality. And that means they're a kind of thought, lacking the crucial sensory aspects of perception.

But can thoughts really account for the awareness we have of our conscious states? Rosenthal contends that thoughts, like perceptions, can track features in the environment. Further, they can be triggered automatically, out of our control. Indeed, there are lots of times when we can't help but think certain things, no matter how hard we try not to (don't think of a purple elephant!). But what about all the fine-grained detail we can be aware of in conscious experience? Doesn't that point to a perception-like process? Rosenthal argues against the claim that we lack the concepts to make us aware of all we experience consciously. First, we should remember that concepts are not words – just because we lack a word for something does not mean we lack a concept for it. Forgetting this sometimes makes thought seem much too thin. Secondly, we can greatly increase the range of our concepts by thinking *comparatively*, in terms of lighter than, darker than, hotter than, and so on. So even if we lack a specific concept for a shade of red, we can pick it out conceptually as something slightly lighter than brick red or slightly darker than crimson. And, finally, we need to keep in mind that there may be much less to represent consciously than we sometimes think. As the "extended" theorists like Alva Noë argue (see chapter 6), we have no need to consciously represent all the detail we track. Rather, we have it available and can represent it if needed. Indeed, it turns out that much less of our current visual field is colored than we think. Out on the periphery, we cannot distinguish colors, even though it doesn't seem that color fades out at the edges of what we see.[7] Taken together, Rosenthal contends, there is no reason to reject a thought model for higher-order awareness. And given the higher-order qualities problem of the HOP view, a HOT approach seems the one to take. This gives us the flavor of the traditional higher-order view.[8] We'll consider objections to it below, but first we'll lay out the other two versions of the approach, starting with the "self-representational" theory.

The Self-Representational Theory

The traditional higher-order approach holds that the first-order representation and the higher-order awareness of it are realized in distinct states. Further, the approach is committed to a functionalist-informational tracking story, where representation is ultimately unpacked in causal terms. But this opens up a possible problem for the view. What happens if the higher-order state is caused in the wrong way? That is, what if the higher-order state *misrepresents* the first-order state it is about? For example, what if we have a first-order representation of a green field but we mistakenly higher-order represent ourselves as seeing a red carpet instead? And what if the higher-order awareness occurs without any lower-order state *at all*? We'll say more about this worry below in the objections section, but it already seems that something odd is going on. The higher-order state is supposed to make the first-order state conscious – but how can it do that if the first-order state isn't even there? There seems to be an implausible disconnect between our conscious state and our awareness of it. This worry, among other things, is a key motivation for the main variant on the higher-order approach, the *self-representational theory* of consciousness. It shares many features with the traditional approach, but it attempts to forge a much tighter link between our conscious states and our awareness of those states.

The self-representational theory accepts the transitivity principle as a starting point, that conscious states are states we are appropriately aware of. And it agrees with the traditional higher-order view that this awareness is best explained by positing a representation making us aware of our conscious state. But self-representationalists reject the idea that the best way to unpack this representational idea is in terms of two distinct states. Instead, they hold that conscious states represent both the world and themselves. There seems to be an immediate worry, however. Such a view involves self-representation. But the representational theory used to provide a reductive explanation of consciousness is a *causal* theory. One thing represents another when it stands in the right causal relationship to that thing. But then self-representation seems to demand that a state cause itself to be represented. And that can't happen because causes must precede their effects. Self-representation appears to require a special, nonreductive sort of representation (if it can be explained at all), undermining the reductive goals of the higher-order approach, one shared by the self-representational theorists we're focused on. What to do?[9]

Both Uriah Kriegel and Rocco Gennaro, the two main proponents of the self-representational approach (as I'm presenting it here),[10] hold that a state can represent itself when one part of the state represents another part of the state. On this approach, a mental state becomes a conscious state when a part that's about the world ("there's a red ball") unites with a part about the world-directed part ("this very state is representing a red ball"), thereby making the overall complex conscious. Until the complex is formed, there is no conscious state, but because the *parts* can stand in appropriate causal relations, there is no difficulty with self-causation. And while there are some differences in how the two theorists unpack the machinery of self-representation, both ultimately explain the transitivity principle by positing a single, complex world-and-self-directed representational state. And both see the state as amenable to a reductive explanation in neurological terms.

The resulting view appears to have some advantages over the traditional picture. For one, it seems that we can't get the odd situation of having a higher-order awareness of a state that's not even there. The self-representational view holds that a conscious state doesn't exist unless both bits are present and accounted for. There may still be misrepresentation worries nearby (see below), but it does look like the most jarring case of inner error is avoided. Also, the self-representational approach looks like it gives a better explanation of the seemingly intimate connection between our conscious state and our awareness of it. The traditional HO view splits off the conscious state from our awareness of it, and this may fail to capture the phenomenology. It's not that there's a conscious state and separately I think about it (though this can happen in introspection). Rather, it's that the state of seeing red somehow *just is* my awareness of seeing red. The reductive self-representation approach takes this link seriously, making it an intrinsic, internal part of the conscious state. But this still arguably allows for a reductive explanation of consciousness. There is cake, and we get to eat it, too. Finally, the traditional approach is committed to the idea that an unconscious state, combined with another unconscious state, equals a conscious state. But how can an unconscious state make us aware in the appropriate way? The self-representational approach, by contrast, can say that a conscious state makes us aware of both the world and itself. Since the conscious state is conscious, there is no need to say a nonconscious state makes us conscious. And this seems to respect the uniqueness of consciousness – it's a special kind of process, one looping back on itself in interesting ways. The traditional view is just states monitoring states – that seems too thin. We're left with an enriched functional-representational picture, one that may well have the intuitive grounding and explanatory resources to fend off worries of eliminativism and zombies. But before we let the zombies back into the room, I want to discuss one more variation on the higher-order approach, one blending elements of self-representationalism and global-workspace functionalism. It also has the best acronym of the bunch: higher-order global states, or HOGS.

Higher-Order Global States

The HOGS view, developed by Robert Van Gulick (2004; 2006), accepts that there's something right and important about the transitivity principle. But the approach agrees with the self-representational theory that the traditional view's use of two distinct states is a mistake. But instead of trying to work out a theory of state-parts and connections, the HOGS view focuses on a different conception of self-awareness. Our conscious states, as emphasized by the "extended" theories, are deeply embedded in our environments and bodies. These reciprocal feedback connections instantiate a kind of *implicit* self-awareness. There couldn't be these sorts of embedded connections without there being a subject or point of view to ground the connections to the organism. So the very presence of embedded and embodied conscious states such as ours entails the presence of a kind of self-awareness. Phenomenology arguably supports this point. Our experiences are from a point of view – that perspective is always at least implicit in consciousness. What's more, the things we see in the world are not passive cutouts; rather, they are meaningful and substantial presences *for us*. In addition, the sort of global availability marking conscious states, key to the global workspace view, also carries with it an implied self-awareness. States having this sort of global connectivity imply at least the background presence of an accessing subject who uses the available information. So it may be that a rich enough functionalist theory actually carries with it the sort of inner awareness definitive of the higher-order approach.

Further, Van Gulick argues that the HOGS theory avoids the key problems of the traditional higher-order view. As noted, there is no distinct representing state, so there is no worry about misrepresentation. What's more, there is no trouble with the re-representing of first-order qualitative states in other terms. The first-order states themselves are conscious in virtue of being embedded in complex, implicitly self-aware networks. Finally, the HOGS view inherits the functional plausibility of the global workspace model. In this way, it serves as a kind of "friendly amendment" to the GWS picture, showing how it might fit with the transitivity principle. Van Gulick doesn't see the HOGS view as offering a full-blown strongly reductive explanation of consciousness, one that closes off zombies and the explanatory gap. But he argues that this sort of view is the right sort of step on the road to reduction, providing a comprehensive picture connecting a number of explanatory ideas. So this may not be the whole reductive hog, but it may be HOGS enough.

The higher-order approach in all its variations may offer the richest functional-representational story available to those of us holding out for a reductive theory of consciousness. What's more, its emphasis on self-awareness places it nearby in "theoretical space" to phenomenological approaches to the mind, those championed by Husserl, Heidegger, Sartre, and others.[11] Though phenomenologists generally reject the sort of reductive representational maneuver central to the higher-order approach canvassed here, they tend to agree with the approach's view on the *structure* of consciousness. Both approaches hold that consciousness involves a kind of awareness of oneself as being in this or that state and perhaps also that it involves a kind of "looping" inward- and outward-looking complex. The higher-order approach can therefore point to phenomenological research as a source of support, at least for the data a theory needs to explain.[12] And the commonsense plausibility of the transitivity principle provides some help in fending off charges of "subject changing" by lovers of qualia and "what it's like" (see below). But the view, predictably, has its worries – the philosophical rug always bumps up somewhere!

Worries for the Higher-Order Approach

There are a number of important objections to the higher-order approach in all its forms. One key worry is that the theory makes consciousness too sophisticated (Carruthers 1989; Block 2003). If the higher-order approach is correct, we must have a range of higher-order processes monitoring our first-order states. These processes either issue in a distinct higher-order state (in the traditional view), or work to combine nonconscious state-parts into a complex self-representational state. Either way, it appears we need lots of cognitive machinery. And this may rule out the possibility of simple-minded critters having conscious experience. Just how sophisticated one must be to have conscious states on the view is a matter of debate, but some hold that the metacognitive abilities required for higher-order and self-representational states would rule out all but humans over the age of three from being conscious![13] A range of studies in developmental psychology arguably show that the ability to explicitly think of ourselves and others in mental terms does not emerge until age three and a half or so. At this point, children normally can pass what psychologists call the "false belief task," a task requiring one to recognize that another person might have false beliefs (Wimmer and Perner 1983). But if you don't recognize that others' beliefs might be false, it's not clear you have any ideas what beliefs are. And someone without the concept of belief (and other interrelated concepts) is not really thinking about others in mental terms. But if someone can't think of others in this way, it's not clear why we'd think that they can think of themselves in mental terms. So if there's evidence that thinking in mental terms doesn't emerge until three and a half, then arguably we can't form higher-order states (or state parts), which seem to demand such ability. And that means babies can't have conscious states on the higher-order view, nor can any nonhuman animals, with a few possible exceptions like chimpanzees. While this result is not obviously false or incoherent (indeed, Descartes held something like this view), it's not a happy position to be forced into. It certainly seems like dogs and cats have conscious experiences of some kinds, like pleasures and pains. And surely two-year-old children are conscious! What's more, the higher-order approach is also committed to some level of *self-consciousness*. Again, psychological research challenges the idea that dogs or babies have such sophisticated levels of awareness.[14]

Proponents of the higher-order approach argue that the resources needed to form higher-order states are less substantial than they first appear (Rosenthal 2005; Gennaro 2012; see also Carruthers 2000). All that's needed, arguably, is an ability to make an appearance/reality distinction in thought, not full-blown false-belief attribution. If I can recognize that the world is not always as it seems, I've got at least some grasp of "seeming," and that may be enough to track my own states (in terms of how things seem to me). And the idea of self need not be a rich, reflective conception of who I am as a person. Rather, it just needs to be some way of tracking the difference between me and the world. Even simple animals manage not to eat their own limbs. Further, they can often track their place in a pecking order. And that may be enough to allow for the sort of inner awareness demanded by the higher-order approach. These are empirical issues, so the jury is still out. But note that one of the costs of increasing the sophistication of the processes involved in consciousness is the danger of ruling out the consciousness of simpler minds.

Another key worry for the view is that, in general, being conscious *of* something does not make that *thing* conscious. If I am conscious of a rock, that does not make the rock a conscious rock (Goldman 1993). But we are asked to accept the idea that, if I'm appropriately conscious of my mental state, it does become conscious. Likewise, even in the case of some of my internal states, being aware of them won't make them conscious. I can become conscious of states of my liver, but they don't thereby become conscious liver states. So the very process of transitive consciousness ("consciousness of") at the heart of the higher-order approach seems mysterious and unprecedented. Why should being conscious of a state make it conscious?

In response, defenders of the higher-order approach can point out that it's not merely a matter of being conscious of something. Rather, we must be conscious of *ourselves* as being in that state. Consciousness, in part, is about mental integration on this view. And can I really be conscious of myself as being in a rock state? That seems off. What are we supposed to be aware of in that case? And while perhaps I can in principle become aware of myself as being in this or that liver state, I still need the right sort of access to the state to form the appropriate concepts (or nonconceptual representations) and to spontaneously trigger them in a way that seems direct. Finally, what I'm aware of when I'm aware of my conscious state is states that themselves carry information, that represent things (hence the "higher-order" label). So, I am aware of myself as being in a state representing a red ball or a shrill trumpet. When this occurs, I become aware of myself as being aware of the world in a certain way. And that's what consciousness amounts to, on the higher-order view. When I'm aware of a rock or a nonrepresentational liver state, this iterated awareness definitive of consciousness does not occur. Note, however, that the rock/liver problem seems harder to motivate for the self-representational approach. How could a rock be literally part of my conscious state? And the same response seems to rule out conscious liver states, though a more extended, distributed view of mind might leave this an open question (state parts need not be spatially connected). While it may be that the self-representational view collapses into the traditional approach on closer inspection (see below), to the extent that they differ, the self-representational approach seems to have an advantage on the rock/liver worry.

But what about the looming worry of higher-order misrepresentation?[15] What exactly is supposed to be the problem here? If higher-order misrepresentation can occur, we're faced with the question of what it would be like for the subject in such a case. Consider a case where the first-order state visually represents a red ball and the higher-order state represents us as seeing a green ball. What would it be like for the subject? According to the traditional higher-order view, it's most plausible that the higher-order state dictates what it's like for the subject.[16] It makes us aware of the state we're in – it tells us what's going on at the first-order level. So if it tells us we're seeing a green ball, it's not clear how we could be aware of anything else, on the view. But things get worse. Imagine that we have *no* first-order state occurring, but we have a higher-order state to the effect that we're seeing a green ball. What would it be like then? If we're already committed to the higher-order state dictating what it's like, it looks like we must say that it will seem to the subject that she's seeing a green ball. But then she's in a conscious state, even though the state she's aware of herself as being in *doesn't exist*! Wait, she's in a conscious state that doesn't exist? Surely, a minimal requirement on being a conscious state is that the state exists! Something very weird has happened to the higher-order view.

Some higher-order theorists simply accept this possibility (Rosenthal 2004; Weisberg 2011). If all we mean by "being in a conscious state" is "being aware of yourself as being in this or that state," then so long as you're aware of yourself in the right way, you're in a conscious state. I may take myself to be aware of a tree, even if the tree is not present. And there's even a sense in which I can (perhaps drunkenly) be aware of Santa Claus, even though he doesn't exist. If conscious states are just states we're aware of, then we can be aware of them even when they're not there. On this view, conscious experience is a sort of story we tell ourselves about what's happening in our minds, a representation of the ebb and flow of our first-order states. It's usually an accurate story, but errors can occur. And since all we know about the first-order states comes through the higher-order representation, we would never directly be aware of such errors, explaining, perhaps, why this defense is intuitively hard to swallow.

But in the face of such a jarring result, many higher-order theorists deny the possibility of misrepresentation, at least of the most radical kind. It might be that even a distinct higher-order representation cannot form unless it is causally integrated with a lower-order state. That is, the presence of a lower-order state might be a necessary condition for the forming of a higher-order representation. This would preserve the two-state picture, while rejecting radical misrepresentation where *no* lower-order state is present. Similarly, self-representationalists hold that a conscious state complex cannot form unless both the higher-order and lower-order elements are present (Kriegel 2009). So, by definition, there's no conscious state at all in radical mismatch cases. And some self-representationalists contend that unless an appropriately accurate match occurs between the higher-order and first-order bits, the complex will not occur either (Gennaro 2012). However, it may be that these claims are in conflict with the reductive representationalist flavor of the view. If representation by a higher-order state-part is what makes us aware of our conscious state, and that's what consciousness amounts to (by the transitivity principle), then it's not clear why a mismatch wouldn't still be conscious, or, more seriously, why the right sort of higher-order element *on its own* wouldn't suffice to make us conscious. We'd be aware of the same things as we are in "veridical" experience, right? And in the veridical case, it's the higher-order state-part that dictates what we're aware of. So we're left worrying that the self-representational view hasn't distanced itself effectively from the traditional view, at least with respect to this problem.[17]

So far, it may seem that the HOGS view emerges unscathed. It avoids the dogs/babies worry by making the higher-order awareness implicit, as something present in a range of embedded, reciprocal representational relationships. These can be had by states of animals and babies, plausibly. Further, rocks and liver states do not enter into these kinds of complex feedback loops, so that problem is avoided as well. Finally, because there isn't an explicit representation by a distinct state or state-part, there is no worry about misrepresentation. You've got to represent to misrepresent. But the cost of these benefits may be that the implicit self-awareness of HOGS is too thin to account for experience. Recall that implicit self-awareness emerges from the rich feedback-laden interactions we have mentally with our bodies and our environment. The stability of these "loops" implies the background presence of a self, of an agent. But many *nonconscious* processes display the complex embedded structure indicative of implicit self-awareness. For example, I may walk through a densely wooded environment while engaged in deep thought. I am often unaware of my surroundings in such cases, even though there must be the complex feedback-influenced adjustment marking the implicit self-awareness posited in HOGS. Indeed, many of the motor skills we use constantly are rife with implicit self-awareness, though they are usually nonconscious. If you become conscious of your feet while you dance, you're probably about to trip!

HOGS theory replies that it's not just any implicit self-awareness at work. Rather, it's the rich implicit self-awareness of states in a global workspace. Since these other processes involving implicit self-awareness do not engage the global workspace, they are not conscious. But this seems to push the view back towards the functionalist, rather than the higher-order, camp. Indeed, it is hard to see how implicit self-awareness could explain the transitivity principle in the first place, if it's present in so many processes that intuitively we are not conscious of. This is not to say the view is false. Rather, it just may not capture the data that the higher-order approach is really after and instead is perhaps better seen as an enriched version of the GWS theory considered in chapter 6.[18]

But functionalist approaches are plagued by zombies, perhaps knocking HOGS out of the higher-order frying pan and into Chalmers's fire. But does the higher-order approach do any better with zombies? One line of thought is that, if we accept that consciousness is *defined* by the transitivity principle, then zombies are not really conceivable after all. If a creature is appropriately aware of its states, then it's conscious, full stop. And it looks like what Chalmers's calls zombies will be aware in the appropriate way. Indeed, to some ears, if you say, yes, zombies are aware of their mental states in a seemingly direct and spontaneous way, but they're *still* not conscious, it sounds very weird.[19] Or maybe we should allow that zombies are prima facie conceivable, but, once we all realize that the transitivity principle is the best way to characterize consciousness, we'll see that this was premature. But how can we tell if the transitivity principle has things right? And isn't it just subject changing – that is, cheating – to simply *assert* that the transitivity principle is the way to go?

Well, we've come around full circle here: how *do* we define consciousness, anyway? Perhaps we should be more open-minded and less dogmatic about that one. Maybe as we learn more about the mind from science, one or another definition of consciousness will seem more plausible. Or maybe we'll just have to give up some of what we now take to be obviously true about consciousness as the empirical results pile up. And then we may take up transitivity as the best fit with both common sense and science, giving some here but saving a bit there. Or maybe at the end of the day, we'll see that transitivity isn't the way to go, and we'll have to kill the zombies some other way, if they can be killed at all. Philosophical zombies, like their monster-movie namesakes, are hard to kill. And therein lies the philosophical fun!

Conclusion

So, after this somewhat twisted journey, what are we left with? It's clear that consciousness poses a range of deep and interesting philosophical questions, questions that promise to remain center stage in debates about the mind. But it's also clear that there is great disagreement among theorists about how to proceed. Some take this conflict as evidence of the futility of tackling this problem, while other see it as a call for radical new thinking. But it may be that what we're observing is the normal mish-mash of proto-scientific theorizing as a difficult area of study gets its initial development. Eventually, a clear path to explaining consciousness may emerge, despite the tangled forest of views marking the current debate.

My own view is one of guarded optimism. As I assume is clear from the text, I am sympathetic with the idea that a strongly reductive view is not dead on arrival, and that we ought to spend our time pushing and developing these sorts of theories as best we can. It may be that we'll never reach the grand goal of an illuminating explanation of consciousness, but we certainly don't know that we can't get there yet, in my humble opinion. What's more, we really have no idea what the future of neuroscience will bring us. We are just beginning in our study of the most complex thing we know of in the universe – the human brain. It shouldn't be a surprise that we haven't got it all worked out yet after only a hundred or so years. If, after another couple of hundred years, we still haven't gotten anywhere, we can then embrace a nonreductive view. By then, no doubt the nonreductivists will have worked out all the metaphysical kinks in their views! In the meantime, there's plenty of philosophical work to do on all sides of the debate.

Further Reading

David Armstrong presents the first contemporary versions of the higher-order view in his 1968 *A Materialist Theory of Mind*. Rosenthal major papers on the HOT theory are collected in his 2005 *Consciousness and Mind*. Lycan defends his view in *Consciousness* and *Consciousness and Experience*. Kriegel's view is presented in his 2009 *Subjective Consciousness: A Self-Representational Theory*; and Gennaro's view is given in *The Consciousness Paradox*. Van Gulick's HOGS is found in his 2004 and 2006 papers. Van Gulick's (2004) also contains an overview of the major criticisms of the traditional higher-order view. See also Block (2011b).

Notes

Chapter 1   The Problem

1 From here on, I'll generally drop the "hard" when I talk about the problem of consciousness. But it should be remembered that that's the focus of the discussion, unless otherwise mentioned.

2 This "what it's like" way of talking makes it into contemporary philosophical jargon from Thomas Nagel's 1974 paper "What is it Like to be a Bat?"

3 The distinction between creature and state consciousness is introduced in Rosenthal's 1986 paper "Two Concepts of Consciousness."

4 See Lewis 1994 or Braddon-Mitchell and Jackson 2006, ch. 1, for example.

5 Unsurprisingly, there is much philosophical debate about what it means to supervene. For our purposes, a rough understanding is enough. Most agree that if A supervenes on B, there cannot be a change in A without a change in B, though not vice versa. I follow Braddon-Mitchell and Jackson 2006 in using the "nothing over and above" way of putting things. For the complexities of this issue see McLaughlin and Bennett 2014.

Chapter 2   Mysterianism

1 See, for example, McGinn's 1993 *Problems in Philosophy: The Limits of Inquiry* for another, more general attempt to establish his mysterian conclusion.

Chapter 3   Dualism

1   Descartes 1984 [1640].
2   Locke 1979 [1689].
3   Though see Foster 1991 for a modern defense of substance dualism.
4   See Braddon-Mitchell and Jackson 2006 for a more detailed treatment of these developments in philosophy of mind.
5   See Chalmers 2010, ch. 6, for a more complex version of the argument, along with an extensive critical analysis of the possible responses to the argument.
6   See Garson 2006 for an excellent introduction to possible ⎱ worlds and modal logic.   ⎰
7   Chalmers notes that the conclusion of the zombie argument is also consistent with versions of neutral monism and panpsychism. See ch. 4.
8   See, for example, Block's response in ch. 5.
9   See Dennett's view in ch. 6.
10   Recent defenders of interactionist dualism include Foster 1991, Hodgson 1991, Lowe 1996, H. Robinson 1982, Stapp 1993, and Swinburne 1986.
11   Another choice philosopher's word: "cause." Since David Hume, this one has been particularly tough to get a grip on!
12   See Collins 2011.
13   See Chalmers 1996, ch. 10.
14   With apologies to Roger Penrose and Stuart Hameroff, who've argued for this sort of position as the best defense of *physicalism* about consciousness. See Penrose 1989; Hameroff and Penrose 2013.
15   The main contemporary defender of the view is William Robinson. See his 1988, 2004. See also Jackson 1982.
16   See Wegner 2003.
17   See also Haggard 2005.

Chapter 4   Nonreductive Views

1   Where I'm using "stuff" in the most general, generic sense. "Schmutz," "what's-it," and "thing-a-ma-bob" have a similar meaning, though they are less dignified.
2   There is also a form of nonreductive physicalism, sometimes called "token" or "supervenient" physicalism. I will touch on that briefly in the next chapter.

3   This way of putting things, as well as much of the substantive material in this chapter, owes a great debt of gratitude to Leopold Stubenberg's wonderful article on neutral monism in the *Stanford Encyclopedia of Philosophy*. See "Further reading."

4   See Spinoza's *Ethics*; Leibniz's *Monadology*; James's *A Pluralistic Universe*; and Russell's *The Analysis of Mind*.

5   Another important related view is that of Derk Pereboom. In his rich 2011 book *Consciousness and the Prospects of Physicalism*, Pereboom presents a version of neutral monism (or something very much like it). Interestingly, he also presents arguments claiming that we don't know all there is to know about consciousness as it's accessed from the first-person perspective. This line of thinking fits well with some of the strongly reductive view we'll look at in chs 6, 7, and 8.

6   Indeed, Strawson holds this is among the craziest ideas to be defended in the history of human thought:

> For this particular denial is the strangest thing that has ever happened in the whole history of human thought, not just the whole history of philosophy. It falls, unfortunately, to philosophy, not religion, to reveal the deepest woo-woo of the human mind. I find this grievous, but, next to this denial, every known religious belief is only a little less sensible than the belief that grass is green (2006: 5–6).

7   Here used in its more technical sense of an independent underlying stuff capable of undergoing change in properties.

8   See Stubenberg 2008, 2013, and Banks 2010, for more on this view.

Chapter 5   The Identity Theory

1   The sort of identity theory I will be discussing is known as "type identity": an identity between types of mental states and types of brain states. I will not be discussing so-called "token identity" theories, like the "anomalous monism" of Donald Davidson, for example. Those views are important in the broader context of the mind–body problem, but have received less focus in the current literature on consciousness. For reasons of space, I leave them out, though they are interesting in their own right. See Davidson 2001[1970]; Kim 1998.

2 One interesting view I will not have space to present is John Searle's. Searle famously argues against forms of artificial intelligence and functionalism. His positive view is that consciousness (and understanding) is a product of the brain. But he is not a straightforward identity theorist. He holds that consciousness is *caused* by the brain, which requires it to be separate. Searle also argues against dualism and the zombie worry. See his 1992 *The Rediscovery of the Mind* and his 1997 *The Mystery of Consciousness*.

3 This "what it's like" terminology is borrowed from Thomas Nagel's 1974 paper "What is it Like to Be a Bat?"

4 See Lawrence Weiskrantz's *Consciousness Lost and Found*.

5 Chalmers 1996; Chalmers and Jackson 2001; Jackson 1998; Lewis 1972, 1994.

6 For details, see Block 2007, section IV.

7 Thanks to David Rosenthal for years of dropping imaginary pianos on my foot!

8 A related version of the identity theory is presented in Chris Hill's 1991 book *Sensations: A Defense of Type Materialism*.

9 This way of looking at meaning and reference is also supported by the seminal work on modal logic by Saul Kripke. See especially Kripke's influential work *Naming and Necessity*.

10 See for example Bickle 1998; Bechtel and Mundale 1999. The material in this section was influenced by John Bickle's excellent *Stanford Encyclopedia of Philosophy* article on multiple realizability. See Bickle 2013.

11 Chalmers 2010, ch. 6.

12 See Block 2002. In this approach, Block is following a number of other theorists, starting with Loar 1997. See also Papineau 1993, 2002; and Perry 2001. For criticisms, see Stoljar 2005; Chalmers 2010, ch. 10.

Chapter 6   Functionalism

1 This is the approach of Lewis 1972, 1994. See also Jackson 1998; Braddon-Mitchell and Jackson 2006.

2 For this approach, see Block 1978 on "empirical functionalism." See also Prinz 2012.

3 See Putnam 1967.

4 There is a further famous worry for machine functionalism, brought out by John Searle in his "Chinese room" thought experiment. It seems that a computer might produce all the right outputs, including "verbal" outputs, without knowing

what the words it is using mean. Searle contends that computers just follow formal "syntactic" programs without having
any access to the semantics – the meanings – of what they're
producing. This challenge focuses on understanding rather
than consciousness, but it is worth mentioning here. See Searle
1980.
5 See Hurley 1998; Noë 2005, 2009.
6 See Fodor 1983 for the classic statement of this view.
7 See Figure 2.1, p. 22.
8 For example, see Steven Pinker's *How the Mind Works* for a
defense of the claim that the mind is "massively modular." But
see Jerry Fodor's *The Mind Doesn't Work that Way* for a
response.
9 See Chalmers 1996, 2010.
10 See O'Regan and Noë 2001 for much more on this approach.
11 Though keep in mind the contrary views of new-wave identity
theorists like Bickle, noted in the last chapter.
12 See ch. 3: 41–2.
13 Admittedly, there aren't enough citizens of China to realize
each neuron. At the time that Block developed his example,
the best estimate of the number of neurons in a brain was
lower! But the point of the example is still clear.

Chapter 7   First-Order Representationalism

1 This is not the only way to characterize representationalism.
Some hold it is a rival or improvement to functionalism.
Further, though I am locating representationalism as "strongly
reductive" there are *nonreductive* versions of representationalism. Leibniz arguably held such a view, as do many in the
phenomenological tradition (see ch. 1: 10–11). Such views
generally hold that representation cannot be explained in physicalist terms and then hold that consciousness is a subspecies
of this kind of representation. See Moran 2000 for a good
overview of phenomenological approaches.
2 I will focus on the details of Dretske's later (1995) work on
the issue. His seminal 1981 *Knowledge and the Flow of Information* is the first shot at a theory and differs in some respects
from his presentation in his 1995 *Naturalizing the Mind*. For
views keeping closer to the letter of the earlier work, see, for
example, Aydede and Güzeldere 2001.
3 For these worries and others, see Fodor 1990.
4 See, for example, Harman 1999.

5   Tye captures his view with the acronym PANIC: poised, abstract, nonconceptual intentional content. If you are representational content of this kind, you are conscious. "Abstract" refers to the fact that we see qualities that can be instantiated in more than one object. See Tye 1995, 2000.

6   This section benefited from two fine critical reviews of Prinz's book: Wu 2013 and Mole 2013.

7   Though you are no longer a naive subject, here's the URL for the video: www.theinvisiblegorilla.com/gorilla_experiment. html.

8   See Rosenthal 2005; Gennaro 2012.

Chapter 8   Higher-Order Representationalism

1   Rosenthal 2005; Armstrong 1968, 1981; Lycan 1987, 1996.

2   Kriegel 2009; Gennaro 2012. Note that Gennaro labels his view a version of the higher-order thought theory, rather than a self-representational theory, but for my purposes his view is better grouped with Kriegel's, due to his rejection of an extrinsic higher-order state. Further, both Gennaro and Kriegel agree that consciousness occurs when a single complex state represents both itself and the world. I follow Kriegel 2009 in calling such a view "self-representationalism" to distinguish it from the older, extrinsic higher-order view. I hope that this does not generate too much confusion and my apologies to Gennaro, who resists this classification.

3   Van Gulick 2004, 2006.

4   See Ögmen and Breitmeyer 2006.

5   For example Brentano 1973 [1874]; Thomasson 2000.

6   See Moran 2000.

7   See Dennett 1991.

8   A closely related theory is Peter Carruthers's dispositional higher-order view. Carruthers holds that we need only be disposed to form HO representations to make our states conscious. We don't actually have to re-represent our first-order states, so long as those states are available to our "mind reading" faculty. The view also has affinities with the self-representationalism, holding that first-order states themselves acquire a self-representational element when they are poised to be "consumed" by the mind-reading system. See Carruthers 2000, 2005 for details.

9   Not all self-representationalists accept that this is a serious worry. Ken Williford, for example, argues that so long as we

do not employ an overly-simple causal model of representation, there is no worry about odd "self-causation." The "teleosemantic" view of Ruth Millikan (1984) or the "consumer semantics" of Peter Carruthers (2000) both arguably avoid the problem and retain their reductive credibility. In Williford's words, the idea of self-representation "is no more mysterious than the idea that on can flagellate oneself" (2006: 112). See Williford's fascinating "The Self-Representational Structure of Consciousness" for this and much more.

10 Again, Gennaro does not label himself as a self-representationalist (he holds that his view is a version of the traditional higher-order thought theory). But the description I give in this section fits Gennaro's view, so I'm grouping him here.

11 See Moran 2000; Gallagher and Zahavi 2012.

12 For a view closely related to the higher-order approaches canvassed here, but more directly engaging with the phenomenological approach (and with current neuroscience), see Thomas Metzinger's complex and interesting "self-model" theory. Metzinger holds that when we have the right sort of model of our mental states – a "phenomenal model of the intentionality relation," or PMIR – we have conscious states. See Metzinger 2004, 2010.

13 See Carruthers 1989.

14 See Bekoff, Allen, and Burghardt 2002 for an overview of this debate.

15 For detailed presentations of this worry, see Byrne 1997; Neander 1998; Levine 2001.

16 Rosenthal 2004.

17 See Weisberg 2008, 2013 for more on this issue.

18 See Weisberg 2008.

19 See for example Gennaro's discussion, 2012, pp. 80–1.

References

Alter, Torin, and Howell, Robert (eds). 2011. *Consciousness and the Mind–Body Problem: A Reader*. New York: Oxford University Press.

Armstrong, David M. 1968. *A Materialist Theory of Mind*. London: Routledge and Kegan Paul.

Armstrong, David M. 1981. "What is Consciousness?" in *The Nature of Mind*. Ithaca, NY: Cornell University Press.

Aydede, Murat, and Güzeldere, Guven. 2001. "Consciousness, Conceivability Arguments, and Perspectivalism: The Dialectics of the Debate." *Communication and Cognition* 34(1–2): 99–122.

Baars, Bernard. 1988. *A Cognitive Theory of Consciousness*. Cambridge: Cambridge University Press.

Baars, Bernard. 1997. *In the Theater of Consciousness*. New York: Oxford University Press.

Banks, Erik C. 2010. "Neutral Monism Reconsidered." *Philosophical Psychology* 23(2): 173–87.

Bechtel, William, and Mundale, Jennifer. 1999. "Multiple Realizability Revisited: Linking Cognitive and Neural States," *Philosophy of Science* 66: 175–207.

Bekoff, Marc, Allen, Colin, and Burghardt, Gordon (eds). 2002. *The Cognitive Animal: Empirical and Theoretical Perspectives on Animal Cognition*. Cambridge, MA: MIT Press.

Bickle, John. 1998. *Psychoneural Reduction: The New Wave*. Cambridge, MA: MIT Press.

Bickle, John. 2013. "Multiple Realizability," in Edward N. Zalta (ed.), *The Stanford Encyclopedia of Philosophy*, available at http://plato.stanford.edu/archives/spr2013/entries/multiple-realizability/, accessed March 19, 2014.

Block, Ned. 1978. "Troubles with Functionalism," in N. Block (ed.), *Readings in the Philosophy of Psychology* (Vol. 1). Cambridge, MA: Harvard University Press.

Block, Ned. 1990. "Inverted Earth," in J. Tomberlin (ed.), *Philosophical Perspectives 4: Action Theory and the Philosophy of Mind*. Atascadero, CA: Ridgeview Publishing.

Block, Ned. 1995. "On a Confusion about a Function of Consciousness." *Behavioral and Brain Sciences* 18(2): 227–47.

Block, Ned. 2002. "The Harder Problem of Consciousness." *Journal of Philosophy* 99(8) (August): 391–425.

Block, Ned. 2003. "Consciousness," in Lynn Nadel (ed.), *Encyclopedia of Cognitive Science*. New York: Nature Publishing Group.

Block, Ned. 2007. *Consciousness, Function, and Representation: Collected Papers (Vol. 1)*. Cambridge, MA: MIT Press.

Block, Ned. 2008. "Consciousness and Cognitive Access." *Proceedings of the Aristotelian Society*, Vol. CVIII, Part 3.

Block, Ned. 2011a. "Perceptual Consciousness Overflows Cognitive Access." *Trends in Cognitive Sciences* 15(12): 567–75.

Block, Ned. 2011b. "The Higher Order Approach to Consciousness is Defunct." *Analysis* 71(3): 419–31.

Block, Ned, and Stalnaker, Robert. 1999. "Conceptual Analysis, Dualism, and the Explanatory Gap." *Philosophical Review* 108: 1–46.

Block, N., Flanagan, O., and Güzeldere, G. (eds), *The Nature of Consciousness: Philosophical Debates*. Cambridge, MA: MIT Press.

Braddon-Mitchell, David, and Jackson, Frank. 2006. *Philosophy of Mind and Cognition*, 2nd edn. Oxford: Wiley-Blackwell.

Brentano, Franz. 1973 [1874]. *Psychology from an Empirical Standpoint*. London: Routledge.

Byrne, Alex. 1997. "Some like it HOT: Consciousness and Higher-Order Thoughts." *Philosophical Studies* 86:103–29.

Carruthers, Peter. 1989. "Brute Experience." *Journal of Philosophy* 86: 258–69.

Carruthers, Peter. 2000. *Phenomenal Consciousness*. Cambridge: Cambridge University Press.

Carruthers, Peter. 2005. *Consciousness: Essays from a Higher-Order Perspective*. New York: Oxford University Press.

Chabris, Christopher, and Simons, Daniel. 2009. *The Invisible Gorilla: How Our Intuitions Deceive Us*. New York: Crown Publishing.

Chalmers, David J. 1996. *The Conscious Mind: In Search of a Fundamental Theory*. Oxford: Oxford University Press.

Chalmers, David J. 2010. *The Character of Consciousness*. New York: Oxford University Press.

Chalmers, David J. 2013. "Panpsychism and Panprotopsychism." The Amherst Lecture in Philosophy 8: 1–35. Available at www.amherstlecture.org/chalmers2013.

Chalmers, David J., and Jackson, Frank. 2001. "Conceptual Analysis and Reductive Explanation." *Philosophical Review* 110: 315–61.

Churchland, Patricia S. 1986. *Neurophilosophy: Toward a Unified Science of the Mind–Brain*. Cambridge, MA: MIT Press.

Churchland, Patricia S. 1996. "The Hornswoggle Problem." *Journal of Consciousness Studies* 3(5–6): 402–8.

Clark, Austen. 1993. *Sensory Qualities*. Oxford: Clarendon Press.

Cohen, Michael A., and Dennett, Daniel C. 2011. "Consciousness cannot be Separated from Function." *Trends in Cognitive Sciences* 15(8): 358–64.

Collins, R. 2011. "Energy of the Soul," in M. C. Baker and S. Goetz (eds), *The Soul Hypothesis*. London: Continuum.

Davidson, Donald. 2001 [1970]. "Mental Events," in *Essays on Actions and Events*, 2nd edn. Oxford: Clarendon Press.

Dehaene, Stanislas, and Naccache, Lionel. 2001. "Towards a Cognitive Neuroscience of Consciousness: Basic Evidence and a Workspace Framework." *Cognition* 79: 1–37.

Dennett, Daniel C. 1978. "Toward a Cognitive Theory of Consciousness," in C. Wade Savage (ed.), *Perception and Cognition: Issues in the Foundations of Psychology, Minnesota Studies in the Philosophy of Science IX*. Minneapolis: University of Minnesota Press.

Dennett, Daniel C. 1991. *Consciousness Explained*. Boston: Little Brown.

Dennett, Daniel C. 2005. *Sweet Dreams*. Cambridge, MA: MIT Press.

Descartes, René. 1984 [1640]. "Meditations on First Philosophy," in J. Cottingham, R. Stoothoff, and D. Murdoch (trans.), *The Philosophical Writings of Descartes: Vol. 2*. Cambridge: Cambridge University Press, pp. 1–50.

Dretske, Fred I. 1981. *Knowledge and the Flow of Information*. Cambridge, MA: MIT Press.

Dretske, Fred I. 1995. *Naturalizing the Mind*. Cambridge, MA: MIT Press.

Flanagan, Owen. 1991. *The Science of the Mind*, 2nd edn. Cambridge, MA: MIT Press.

Fodor, Jerry A. 1983. *The Modularity of Mind: An Essay on Faculty Psychology*. Cambridge, MA: MIT Press.

Fodor, Jerry A. 1990. *A Theory of Content and Other Essays*. Cambridge, MA: MIT Press.

Fodor, Jerry A. 2001. *The Mind Doesn't Work That Way: The Scope and Limits of Computational Psychology*. Cambridge, MA: MIT Press.

Foster, John. 1991. *The Immaterial Self: A Defence of the Cartesian Dualist Conception of Mind*. London: Routledge.

Gallagher, Shaun, and Zahavi, Daniel. 2012. *The Phenomenological Mind*, 2nd edn. New York: Routledge.

Garson, James. 2006. *Modal Logic for Philosophers*. Cambridge: Cambridge University Press.

Gennaro, Rocco J. 2012. *The Consciousness Paradox: Consciousness, Concepts, and Higher-Order Thoughts*. Cambridge, MA: MIT Press.

Goldman, Alvin. 1993. "Consciousness, Folk Psychology, and Cognitive Science." *Consciousness and Cognition* 2: 364–82.

Haggard, Patrick. 2005. "Conscious Intention and Motor Cognition." *Trends in Cognitive Sciences* 9(6): 290–5.

Hameroff, Stuart, and Penrose, Roger. 2013. "Consciousness in the Universe: A Review of the 'Orch OR' Theory." *Physics of Life Reviews*. Available at http://dx.doi.org/10.1016/j.plrev.2013.08.002, accessed March 19, 2014.

Harman, Gilbert. 1990. "The Intrinsic Quality of Experience," in J. Tomberlin (ed.), *Philosophical Perspectives, 4: Action Theory and the Philosophy of Mind*. Atascadero, CA: Ridgeview Publishing.

Harman, Gilbert. 1999. *Reasoning, Meaning, and Mind*. Oxford: Clarendon Press.

Hill, Christopher S. 1991. *Sensations: A Defense of Type Materialism*. Cambridge: Cambridge University Press.

Hodgson, D. 1991. *The Mind Matters: Consciousness and Choice in a Quantum World*. Oxford: Oxford University Press.

Hurley, Susan. 1998. *Consciousness in Action*. Cambridge, MA: Harvard University Press.

Jackendoff, Ray. 1987. *Consciousness and the Computational Mind. Explorations in Cognitive science, No. 3*. Cambridge, MA: MIT Press.

Jackson, Frank. 1982. "Epiphenomenal Qualia." *Philosophical Quarterly* 32: 127–36.

Jackson, Frank. 1998. *From Metaphysics to Ethics: A Defence of Conceptual Analysis*. Oxford: Clarendon.

James, William. 1909. *A Pluralistic Universe: Hibbert Lectures at Manchester College on the Present Situation in Philosophy*. New York: Longmans, Green and Co.

Kim, Jaegwon. 1998. *Mind in a Physical World: An Essay on the Mind–Body Problem and Mental Causation*. Cambridge, MA: MIT Press.

Kriegel, Uriah. 2009. *Subjective Consciousness: A Self-Representational Theory*. Oxford: Oxford University Press.

Kripke, Saul. 1980. *Naming and Necessity*. Cambridge, MA: Harvard University Press.

Leibniz, Gottfried W. 1989 [1714]. *Monadology*, in R. Ariew and D. Garber (eds and trans.), *G. W. Leibniz: Philosophical Essays*. Indianapolis: Hackett Publishing Company.

Levine, Joseph. 2001. *Purple Haze: The Puzzle of Consciousness*. Oxford: Oxford University Press.

Lewis, David K. 1972. "Psychophysical and Theoretical Identifications." *Australasian Journal of Philosophy* 50(3) (December): 249–58.

Lewis, David K. 1988. "What Experience Teaches." *Proceedings of the Russellian Society of the University of Sydney*, reprinted in W. Lycan (ed.), *Mind and Cognition*, Oxford: Blackwell, 1990, pp. 499–519.

Lewis, David K. 1994. "Reduction of Mind," in D. Lewis, *Papers in Metaphysics and Epistemology*. Cambridge: Cambridge University Press, pp. 291–324.

Libet, Benjamin. 1985. "Unconscious Cerebral Initiative and the Role of Conscious Will in Voluntary Action." *Behavioral and Brain Sciences* 8(4): 529–39.

Loar, Brian. 1997. "Phenomenal States," in N. Block, O. Flanagan, and G. Güzeldere (eds), *The Nature of Consciousness: Philosophical Debates*. Cambridge, MA: MIT Press.

Locke, John. 1979 [1689]. *An Essay Concerning Human Understanding*. Oxford: Clarendon Press.

Lowe, E. J. 1996. *Subjects of Experience*. Cambridge: Cambridge University Press.

Lycan, William G. 1987. *Consciousness*. Cambridge, MA: MIT Press.

Lycan, William G. 1996. *Consciousness and Experience*. Cambridge, MA: MIT Press.

Mack, Arien, and Rock, Irving. 1989. *Inattentional Blindness*. Cambridge, MA: MIT Press.

Marr, David. 1982. *Vision: A Computational Investigation into the Human Representation and Processing of Visual Information*. San Francisco: W. H. Freeman & Co.

McGinn, Colin. 1993. *Problems in Philosophy: The Limits of Inquiry*. Oxford: Blackwell.

McGinn, Colin. 1999. *The Mysterious Flame: Conscious Minds in a Material World*. New York: Basic Books.

McLaughlin, Brian, and Bennett, Karen. 2014. "Supervenience," in Edward N. Zalta (ed.), *The Stanford Encyclopedia of Philosophy*

(Spring 2014 edn). Available at http://plato.stanford.edu/archives/spr2014/entries/supervenience/, accessed March 19, 2014.

Merikle, P. M., Smilek, D., and Eastwood, J. D. 2001. "Perception without Awareness: Perspectives from Cognitive Psychology." *Cognition* 79: 115–34.

Metzinger, Thomas. 2004. *Being No One: The Self-Model Theory of Subjectivity.* Cambridge, MA: MIT Press.

Metzinger, Thomas. 2010. *The Ego Tunnel: The Science of the Mind and the Myth of the Self.* New York: Basic Books.

Millikan, Ruth G. 1984. *Language, Thought, and Other Biological Categories: New Foundations for Realism.* Cambridge, MA: MIT Press.

Mole, Christopher. 2013. "Review of Jesse J. Prinz, *The Conscious Brain: How Attention Engenders Experience.*" *Notre Dame Philosophical Reviews.* Available at http://ndpr.nd.edu/news/36606-the-conscious-brain-how-attention-engenders-experience/, accessed March 4, 2014.

Moran, Dermot. 2000. *Introduction to Phenomenology.* New York and London: Routledge.

Nagel, Thomas. 1974. "What is it Like to be a Bat?" *Philosophical Review* 83: 435–45.

Nagel, Thomas. 1986. *The View from Nowhere.* New York: Oxford University Press.

Nagel, Thomas. 2012. *Mind and Cosmos: Why the Materialist Neo-Darwinian Conception of Nature Is Almost Certainly False.* New York: Oxford University Press.

Neander, Karen. 1998. "The Division of Phenomenal Labor: A Problem for Representational Theories of Consciousness." *Philosophical Perspectives* 12: 411–34.

Noë, Alva. 2005. *Action in Perception.* Cambridge, MA: MIT Press.

Noë, Alva. 2008. "Life is the Way the Animal is in the World: A Talk with Alva Noë." Edge.org. Available at http://edge.org/conversation/life-is-the-way-the-animal-is-in-the-world, accessed March 4, 2014.

Noë, Alva. 2009. *Out of Our Heads: Why You Are Not Your Brain, and Other Lessons from the Biology of Consciousness.* New York: Hill and Wang.

Ögmen, Haluk, and Breitmeyer, Bruno G. (eds). 2006. *The First Half Second: The Microgenesis and Temporal Dynamics of Unconscious and Conscious Visual Processes.* Cambridge, MA: MIT Press.

O'Regan, J. Kevin, and Noë, Alva. 2001. "A Sensorimotor Account of Vision and Visual Consciousness." *Behavioral and Brain Sciences* 24: 939–1031.

Papineau, David. 1993. "Physicalism, Consciousness, and the Antipathetic Fallacy." *Australasian Journal of Philosophy* 71: 169–83.

Papineau, David. 2002. *Thinking about Consciousness*. Oxford: Oxford University Press.

Penrose, Roger. 1989. *The Emperor's New Mind: Concerning Computers, Minds, and the Laws of Physics*. Oxford: Oxford University Press.

Pereboom, Derk. 2011. *Consciousness and the Prospects of Physicalism*. New York: Oxford University Press.

Perry, John. 2001. *Knowledge, Possibility, and Consciousness*. Cambridge, MA: MIT Press.

Pinker, Steven. 1997. *How the Mind Works*. New York: W. W. Norton and Co.

Prinz, Jesse. 2012. *The Conscious Brain: How Attention Engenders Experience*. New York: Oxford University Press.

Putnam, Hilary. 1967. "The Nature of Mental States." Reprinted in *Mind, Language and Reality. Philosophical Papers, Vol. 2* (1975). Cambridge: Cambridge University Press, pp. 429–40.

Putnam, Hilary. 1975. "The Meaning of 'Meaning,'" in K. Gunderson (ed.), *Language, Mind and Knowledge, Minnesota Studies in the Philosophy of Science, VII*. Minneapolis: University of Minnesota Press.

Quine, Willard Van Orman. 1951. "Two Dogmas of Empiricism." *Philosophical Review* 60: 20–43.

Revonsuo, Antti. 2010. *Consciousness: The Science of Subjectivity*. New York: Psychology Press.

Robinson, Howard. 1982. *Matter and Sense*. Cambridge: Cambridge University Press.

Robinson, William S. 1988. *Brains and People: An Essay on Mentality and its Causal Conditions*. Philadelphia: Temple University Press.

Robinson, William S. 2004. *Understanding Phenomenal Consciousness*. Cambridge: Cambridge University Press.

Rosenthal, David M. 1986. "Two Concepts of Consciousness." *Philosophical Studies* 49(3) (May): 329–59.

Rosenthal, David M. 2004. "Varieties of Higher-order Theory," in R. J. Gennaro (ed.), *Higher-Order Theories of Consciousness*, Amsterdam: John Benjamins, pp. 9–44.

Rosenthal, David M. 2005. *Consciousness and Mind*. Oxford: Clarendon Press.

Russell, Bertrand. 1978 [1921]. *The Analysis of Mind* (reprinted). London: George Allen & Unwin.

Russell, Bertrand. 1992 [1948]. *Human Knowledge: Its Scope and Limits*. London: Routledge.

Schacter, Daniel. 1989. "On the Relation between Memory and Consciousness: Dissociable Interactions and Conscious Experience," in H. Roediger and F. Craik (eds), *Varieties of Memory and Consciousness: Essays in Honour of Endel Tulving*. Mahwah, NJ: Erlbaum.

Schwartz, Stephen. 2012. *A Brief History of Analytic Philosophy: From Russell to Rawls*. Oxford: Wiley-Blackwell.

Seager, William. 1999. *Theories of Consciousness: An Introduction and Assessment*. London and New York: Routledge.

Searle, John. 1980. "Minds, Brains, and Programs." *Behavioral and Brain Sciences* 3(3): 417–57.

Searle, John. 1992. *The Rediscovery of the Mind*. Cambridge, MA: MIT Press.

Searle, John. 1997. *The Mystery of Consciousness*. New York: New York Review of Books.

Shear, Jonathan (ed.). 1997. *Explaining Consciousness: The Hard Problem*. Cambridge, MA: MIT Press.

Smart, J. J. C. 1959. "Sensations and Brain Processes." *The Philosophical Review* 68(2): 141–56.

Sommers, Tamler. 2002. "Of Zombies, Color Scientists, and Floating Iron Bars." *PSYCHE* 8(22) (November).

Sperling, George. 1960. "The Information Available in Brief Visual Presentations." *Psychological Monographs* 74: 1–29.

Spinoza, Baruch. 1985 [1677]. *Ethics*, in E. Curley (ed. and trans.), *The Collected Works of Spinoza*. Princeton: Princeton University Press.

Stapp, H. 1993. *Mind, Matter, and Quantum Mechanics*. Berlin: Springer-Verlag.

Stoljar, Daniel. 2001. "Two Conceptions of the Physical." *Philosophy and Phenomenological Research* 62: 253–81.

Stoljar, Daniel. 2005. "Physicalism and Phenomenal Concepts." *Mind and Language* 20(5): 469–94.

Stoljar, Daniel. 2006. *Ignorance and Imagination: The Epistemic Origin of the Problem of Consciousness*. Oxford: Oxford University Press.

Strawson, Galen. 1994. *Mental Reality*. Cambridge, MA: MIT Press.

Strawson, Galen. 2006. "Realistic Monism: Why Physicalism Entails Panpsychism." *Journal of Consciousness Studies* 13(10–11): 3–31.

Stubenberg, Leopold. 2008. "Neutral Monism: A Miraculous, Incoherent, and Mislabeled Doctrine?," *Reduction and Elimination in the Philosophy of Science. Contributions of the Austrian Ludwig Wittgenstein Society* XVI: 337–9.

Stubenberg, Leopold. 2013. "Neutral Monism," in Edward N. Zalta (ed.), *The Stanford Encyclopedia of Philosophy* (Winter

edn). Available at http://plato.stanford.edu/archives/win2013/
entries/neutral-monism/, accessed March 19, 2014.

Swinburne, Richard. 1986. *The Evolution of the Soul*. Oxford:
Oxford University Press.

Thomasson, Amie L. 2000. "After Brentano: A One-Level Theory
of Consciousness." *European Journal of Philosophy* 8(2):
190–209.

Tye, Michael. 1995. *Ten Problems of Consciousness*. Cambridge,
MA: MIT Press.

Tye, Michael. 2000. *Consciousness, Color, and Content*. Cambridge, MA: MIT Press.

Van Gulick, Robert. 2004. "Higher-Order Global States HOGS: An
Alternative Higher-Order Model of Consciousness," in R. J.
Gennaro (ed.), *Higher-Order Theories of Consciousness: An
Anthology*. Amsterdam and Philadelphia: John Benjamins.

Van Gulick, Robert. 2006. "Mirror Mirror – Is That All?" in Uriah
Kriegel and Kenneth Williford (eds), *Self-Representational
Approaches to Consciousness*. Cambridge, MA: MIT Press.

Varela, Francisco. 1996. "Neurophenomenology: A Methodologi-
cal Remedy for the Hard Problem." *Journal of Consciousness
Studies* 3(4) (June): 330–49.

Wegner, Daniel M. 2003. *The Illusion of Conscious Will*. Cambridge, MA: Bradford/MIT.

Weisberg, Josh. 2008. "Same Old, Same Old: The Same-Order
Representation Theory of Consciousness and the Division of
Phenomenal Labor." *Synthese* 160(2): 161–81.

Weisberg, Josh. 2011. "Misrepresenting Consciousness." *Philosophical Studies* 154 (July): 409–33.

Weisberg, Josh. 2013. "A Problem of Intimacy: Commentary on
Rocco Gennaro's *The Consciousness Paradox*." *Journal of Consciousness Studies* 20(11–12): 69–81.

Weiskrantz, Lawrence. 1999. *Consciousness Lost and Found: A
Neuropsychological Exploration*. New York: Oxford University
Press.

Williford, Kenneth. 2006. "The Self-Representational Structure of
Consciousness," in Uriah Kriegel and Kenneth Williford (eds),
Self-Representational Approaches to Consciousness. Cambridge,
MA: MIT Press.

Wilson, Timothy D. 2002. *Strangers to Ourselves: Discovering the
Adaptive Unconscious*. Cambridge, MA: Harvard/Belknap.

Wimmer, H., and Perner, J. 1983. "Beliefs about Beliefs: Representation and Constraining Function of Wrong Beliefs in Young Children's Understanding of Deception." *Cognition* 13(1): 103–28.

Wu, Wayne. 2013. "Review of *The Conscious Brain: How Attention Engenders Experience* by Jesse Prinz." *Mind*. First published
online: November 28. Available at doi: 10.1093/mind/fzt101

Index